STUDIES IN
THE PHILOSOPHY OF KIERKEGAARD

STUDIES
IN THE PHILOSOPHY OF
KIERKEGAARD

by

E. D. KLEMKE

MARTINUS NIJHOFF – THE HAGUE – 1976

To

A. J. Shakeshaft

ISBN 90 247 1852 X

PRINTED IN THE NETHERLANDS

PREFACE

In this volume, I have given attention to what I consider to be some of the central problems and topics in the philosophical thought of Søren Kierkegaard. Some of the chapters have been previously published but were revised for their appearance here. Others were written expressly for this book. I have tried to focus on issues which have not been customarily dealt with or emphasized in the scholarship on Kierkegaard with the exception of the writings of David Swenson and Paul L. Holmer to which (and to whom) I am greatly indebted. Some of the positions for which I have argued in this volume (especially in Chapters IV and V) may be controversial.

I am grateful to all those who enabled me to carry out or influenced me in my studies of Kierkegaard or who assisted with regard to the research for or preparation of this volume. Among these are: Professors Paul L. Holmer, F. Arthur Jacobson, and Dennis A. Rohatyn; Dean Wallace A. Russell and Vice President Daniel J. Zaffarano of Iowa State University.

E.D.K.

CONTENTS

CHAPTER I

SOME MISINTERPRETATIONS OF KIERKEGAARD

One cannot help being somewhat chagrined over the fact that the more widely Kierkegaard's works are translated and read, the greater is the extent to which the Danish author is misunderstood, caricatured, and falsified. Thus so eminent a philosopher as H. J. Paton has, in a single paragraph of *The Modern Predicament*,[1] issued a series of misinterpretations which are typical of the assertions which have been made by many writers who have read Kierkegaard's works in too cursory a fashion – or perhaps not at all! In the following remarks, I shall not attempt merely to refute Prof. Paton. Rather, I shall use his charges to illustrate the general kinds of remarks which are frequently made about Kierkegaard. Similar misinterpretations have appeared in many works, but seldom have they been so neatly assembled in one paragraph.

I

The section in which the pertinent paragraph appears is entitled "The way of absurdity." Prof. Paton discusses various paths with regard to religious matters. One of these is the way of absurdity, which is described as: "Not merely to abandon thinking, but to spurn and deride it, to welcome paradox and to glorify inconsistency."[2] After briefly mentioning Martin Luther as being a representative of this view, Prof. Paton then states: "This rejection of reason finds its most elaborate modern expression in the voluminous writings of Kierkegaard, and his popularity today is a sign of the dangerous pass to

[1] H. J. Paton, *The Modern Predicament* (London: George Allen and Unwin Ltd.; N.Y.: the Macmillan Co., 1955).
[2] *Ibid.*, p. 119.

which we have come – a mark of desperation and despair."[3] Prof.
Paton then lists several theses to support this view, all of which may
be seen to be misinterpretations by the discerning students of Kierkegaard. I shall list the theses in Prof. Paton's words, and in the order
in which he presents them, and then attempt to clarify the various
misunderstandings.

　　I. Kierkegaard wrote "before the development of Biblical criticism;
and he shows no interest in science or in the bearing of science on
religion."

　　If the reference to biblical criticism is meant to imply that Kierkegaard was a literalist with respect to the interpretations of Christian
doctrine, then the charge is untrue, as this kind of pseudo-objective
approach to religious beliefs is precisely what Kierkegaard decries.
More important here is the suggestion that Kierkegaard was unaware
of the development of modern biblical criticism, as a scholarly enterprise. While he rarely mentions the authors of the biblical criticism
movement, a close reading of such works as the *Concluding Unscientific
Postscript* shows that Kierkegaard was certainly aware of the achievements in this field.[4] In fact, he often employs aspects of the critical
method himself, and is thus a kind of representative of the view.[5]
This is not to suggest that Kierkegaard slavishly aligned himself with
the critical enterprise. For he realized that even if the biblical critics
succeeded in their task – whether it be the authenticating of the
Scriptures or the opposite – this still would not settle what Kierkegaard held to be the primary religious question, namely, "What does
it mean for me to be a Christian?"[6]

　　We have yet to consider the charge that Kierkegaard shows no
interest in science or in the bearing of science on religion. It might be
more accurate to characterize Kierkegaard's writings as *resulting from*
the bearing of science on religion. That is, Kierkegaard was aware of
the fact that the achievements of the various sciences – and scholarship
in general – invalidated certain religious views which had been traditionally held. It was partly this fact which led him to seek a new locus
for religious truth, in the personality of a man rather than in the
objective realm. The methodology of the sciences, he held, was ap-

---

　　[3] *Ibid.*, p. 120. The remaining quotations from Prof. Paton's book all occur on page 120.
　　[4] Walter Lowrie points out that one of the arguments of *The Sickness Unto Death* is
directed against the doctrine of David Strauss's *Leben Jesu*. See p. 225, note.
　　[5] See, e.g., S. Kierkegaard, *Concluding Unscientific Postscript* Transl. by D. F. Swenson
& W. Lowrie (Princeton: Princeton Press, 1944) pp. 25f.
　　[6] *Ibid.*, pp. 29–35.

propriate to the kind of endeavors which are within the province of science. He had no quarrel with the findings in biology, astronomy, etc. But it was the attempt to use the scientific methodology in the "sphere of the spirit" that Kierkegaard denounced. For the effort to attain to objectivity with respect to the essential mark of humanity, namely, personality, weakened the ethical and religious passion of men.[7]

In short, Kierkegaard recognized that in the pursuit of science and scholarship it is essential for the observer to be objective and disinterested.[8] The aim of science and scholarship is the attainment of an objective truth with varying degrees of certainty (maximum certainty in logic and mathematics; wide ranges of probability in science, history, and common observation). But again, Kierkegaard simply pointed out that that which is appropriate to one kind of pursuit may be inappropriate to another kind. Since, as he thought, Christianity is "an affair of the spirit," it is also, therefore, a matter of subjectivity and inwardness. In this realm, no objective certainty is possible. In fact, it is a mistake even to attempt to seek objective assurance in these matters.[9]

We may therefore conclude that the charge that Kierkegaard was *ignorant* of matters pertaining to science and scholarship – whether with respect to the Bible or to the world – is clearly false. However, the assertion that Kierkegaard shows no interest in the bearing of science on religion is just as clearly true. But this statement must be clarified, as it is above. Otherwise a misleading effect is created. Actually, a close reading of Kierkegaard's works leads one to be amazed at the degree to which Kierkegaard was aware of, and entered into a discussion of, matters which have been credited to discussion in more recent years.[10]

2. "The rationalism threatening religion he found principally ... in the philosophy of Hegel and his followers."

It is certainly true that Kierkegaard's polemic was frequently directed against Hegel and the type of speculation which was characteristic of the Hegelian Philosophy. But to say that Kierkegaard held Hegelian rationalism to be the principal rationalistic threat to religion is an exaggeration. He looked upon Hegel and the Hegelian philosophy – with its "recitation of paragraphs" and the promise that everything

---

[7] S. Kierkegaard, *Journal*, VII A 186, 187–200; X A 73; partially quoted in the *Postscript*, p. xv.

[8] *Postscript*, p. 70, footnote; p. 85.

[9] *Ibid.*, pp. 41ff.

[10] The tautological nature of analytic sentences and the distinction between cognitive and emotive meaning are suggested throughout the *Postscript*.

will become clear at the end – as comical, rather than a threat. In nearly all the references to Hegel, Kierkegaard seems disappointed that so much talent and careful scholarship should be expended upon so fruitless a task. Kierkegaard genuinely admired Hegel's intellectual ability. He once said that Hegel's system would be the greatest philosophical work ever created, if Hegel had admitted that it was merely a hypothesis. The latter's failure to admit this and his claim to have stated truths which possessed objective certainty led Kierkegaard to construe him as an essentially comic figure.[11]

It is perhaps appropriate to mention that if any movements appeared as a threat to religion, for Kierkegaard, they were the culture accommodation of Grundtvig and the "Churchianity" characteristic of Bishops Martensen and Mynster. For in these movements Kierkegaard saw what he later called the disappearance of Christianity from Christendom.[12]

3. Kierkegaard "denies any objective basis for religion."

This statement is vague. Kierkegaard does not deny that various attempts have been made to establish the truth of religion, including that of Christianity, on objective grounds. Book One of the *Postscript* is devoted to a consideration of "The Objective Problem Concerning the Truth of Christianity." Kierkegaard is aware of all the arguments which can be elaborated in this type of enterprise. He, too, can give the arguments for the existence of God. He can assemble data by which to attempt to establish religious truth on an objective basis. He shows remarkable skill and detachment in considering the objective problem: "What is Christianity?"

What Kierkegaard denies is that any final and conclusive results can be obtained by this sort of endeavor. For objective truth is of two types: (1) the truth of logic and mathematics, truth concerning ideal entities, or even tautologies; truth which is certain, but does not pertain to anything existent; and (2) the truth of science, common sense observation, and history; truth which pertains to existents, but which is therefore merely probable, and never certain.[13] Most religious thinkers would not wish to say that religious truth consists only of the former, as this would give to God a merely mythical or ideal status. Thus they have pursued the second alternative. But, as has been

---

[11] *Postscript*, p. 558. See also p. 34, footnote.
[12] See, Kierkegaard, *Attack Upon Christendom*, for details. Transl. by W. Lowrie (Princeton: Princeton Press, 1946).
[13] *Postscript*, pp. 38, 99, 134, 169–70.

mentioned, the greatest certainty obtainable in the historical, objective realm is merely an approximation. "And an approximation,"
writes Kierkegaard, "when viewed as a basis for an eternal happiness,
is wholly inadequate."[14]

Kierkegaard therefore maintains that scholarship and learning have
placed the emphasis upon the wrong question. Instead of considering
the objective problem, "What is Chritianity?" one ought, rather, to
stress the subjective problem: "The Relation of the Subject to the
Truth of Christianity," or "How am I to become a Christian?" Thus
Kierkegaard introduces the doctrine of truth as subjectivity. By
subjectivity, Kierkegaard does not mean mere whimsicality. His is not
the view that the truth of religion is established on "grounds" of
wishful thinking or the personal inclinations of each individual apart
from any objective proclamation. Kierkegaard is aware that the
historical proclamation exists. His meditations and prayers reveal this
fact clearly enough.[15]

But the crucial question, as Kierkegaard sees it, is: How may I be
related to this proclamation, or to the possibility for personal transformation which it presents? His answer is: This is a subjective matter.
By this he means that the answer is determined by each subject or
individual upon the basis of his entire selfhood, rather than merely
his intellect. To give assent to the objective doctrine is an intellectual
process. And there is nothing determinatively religious about this.
"Even the devils believe and tremble," etc. The significantly religious
step is taken, according to Kierkegaard, when each subject personally
appropriates the truth of the Christian proclamation by an inward,
decisive act. This act involves the entire being or selfhood of a person,
not merely his intellect. Kierkegaard does not negate the use of the
intellect. On the contrary, he insists that being a self, maximizing one's
capacity as a person, involves more than having views. Being a self also
involves one's passions, interests, and concerns. It is the latter which
are definitive of selfhood.[16]

Thus, to say that Kierkegaard denies any objective basis for religion
is not a significant statement without some explication. This is not
to say that Kierkegaard was necessarily right in his discussion of the
problem. And I am not suggesting that he was. I am merely attempting
to obtain an honest statement of what he, in fact, *said*.

[14] *Ibid.*, p. 25.
[15] See, e.g., *Christian Discourses, Edifying Discourses, The Works of Love, Training in Christianity*, and other religious works.
[16] See *Postscript*, p. 33. This entire volume deals with the objective vs. subjective problem.

4. According to Kierkegaard, "there must be a leap of faith into paradox and absurdity. His motto is *'credo quia absurdum'*; and he carries it to the utmost length."

We now come to one of the most important and controversial topics in the Kierkegaardian literature. Prof. Paton misses the point completely. To say, as he does, that Kierkegaard's motto is *"credo quia absurdum,"* and that "he carries it to the utmost length," is a totally false characterization. Kierkegaard uses the words 'absurd' and 'paradox', but with very special meanings. And if one reads the entire context, and not merely the sentences in which these words appear, one can more readily understand what these meanings are.[17] In the following, I shall consider his use of the word 'paradox', but, with minor alterations in vocabulary, a similar meaning is conveyed by his use of 'absurd'.

When Kierkegaard speaks of the element of paradox (and he does so especially in connection with Christianity, but also in wider contexts), it is important to note a meaning of 'paradox' which he does *not* advocate. This is the logical paradox. And here is the source of much confusion among those who criticize Kierkegaard on this topic. Kierkegaard does *not* maintain that Christianity, for example, should be involved in logical paradoxes; nor does he anywhere suggest that the religious man's language should be logically contradictory. Let us see why this is so.

A logical paradox is the kind of sentence which asserts that contradictories are both true or both false. The logician rightly insists that a paradox of this sort is impossible to reflect upon. It must be strongly maintained that Kierkegaard did *not* fall into this error. He distinguishes a logical paradox from at least two other kinds. He gives no indication that Christianity ought to involve a person in logical paradoxicality. Indeed, he attacks this type of sloppy thinking. For one cannot violate the rules of logic and make sense. Kierkegaard is insistent upon this point. I am convinced that it is only through careless reading that certain commentators have made him an advocate of logical paradoxicality.

What, then, are the senses in which Kierkegaard uses the term 'paradox'?

There is, first, what might be called the *existential paradox*, the paradox which results when one's thought is about what exists.

---

[17] For 'absurd' see *Postscript*, pp. 183–91. For 'paradox' see pp. 186–98, 201–4, 241–2, and many shorter passages. Also *Philosophical Fragments*, chap. 3.

Reflection about matters of fact (as seen in the works of various philosophers) has often claimed to be about that which cannot be reflected, namely, existence. Existence is not a property of reflection. Reflection presupposes it. Every attempt to prove that something *exists* fails. Proofs only have to do with the qualities of things. Reflection may, indeed, involve the affirmation that there is something in existence, in this sense of presupposing it, but reflection cannot produce any existent. This is true whether one is referring to individual objects, the whole world, or God. This fact Kierkegaard calls a paradox.

The paradox here is a limit to reflection. Kierkegaard, one might note, is asserting nothing pious or startling at this point. He merely acknowledges what he sees to be a limit to all acts of intelligence. No illogicality is involved in the matter. And, really, there is nothing new here. For, after all, is he not merely reaffirming Kant's statement that existence is not a predicate?[18]

Another kind of paradox is found in Kierkegaard's writings. It might be called the *behavioral paradox*. Kierkegaard elaborates the meaning of this type of paradox in connection with his discussion of Christianity.

The paradoxicality of Christianity, says Kierkegaard, is a paradox of interests and values, a behavioral paradoxicality.[19] We may best illustrate this by following Kierkegaard's procedure. He refers, throughout the *Philosophical Fragments*, to the Greek tradition, which assumed man as the measure of all things,[20] and which stresses an analogy between the known and the unknown.[21] To make an inference about the unknown, one must do so by analogy with the known, according to some Greek thinkers. God, thus, must be like the known, it was said. His qualities were held to be commensurate with those of man. Incommensurateness was posited only in the negative sense of evil and the demonic.

Kierkegaard noticed that Christians have often pursued this same method of making God commensurate with the main values and aims of man's life. They have defined the principal ends and values of life to be: health, longevity, pleasure, happiness, wealth, etc. This is the sense in which Kierkegaard introduces the terms 'reasonable' and 'unreasonable' and refers to a paradox. The above values are reason-

---

[18] S. Kierkegaard, *Philosophical Fragments*, Transl. by D. F. Swenson (Princeton: Princeton Press, 1946) p. 31. See also *Postscript*, pp. 267–82; p. 290.

[19] *Fragments*, p. 37ff.

[20] *Ibid.*, p. 30.

[21] *Ibid.*, p. 36.

able expectations, to most people. And to advocate living without such values would seem unreasonable to nearly all men. Needless to say, this sense of the term 'reason' differs from rationality in the strict sense. Kierkegaard's point is that most people like to believe that God is somehow commensurate with all the above-mentioned values, and others like them. But the question of importance, as Kierkegaard sees it, is: Is God on the same level with these? According to the New Testament (Kierkegaard points out), God does not necessarily increase one's comfort, pleasure, etc. Here is the paradoxicality of Christianity. It is *not* a paradoxicality which violates the fundamental principles of reason. It is the "paradox" of having one's ordinary sense of values and interests *disturbed* by "encountering" God in Christ. This act creates an opposition within an individual – a behavioral opposition, not a logical one. And because of it, one may acquire a new set of values if one's life is sufficiently disturbed. For Kierkegaard, then, one cannot add God in Christ to the pattern of values already existing. This would be paganism.

However, one need not accept the Christian alternative. Kierkegaard believes that there are two equally significant responses to the awareness of the paradox. The first is to say: "I will change my interests to fit the Christian interests." This Kierkegaard calls the "happy relation of faith." One yields one's interests to the Christian demand. The second kind of response is to say: "No, I choose my own. I am offended by the Christian interest." The latter was the choice made by Nietzsche, whom, I am sure, Kierkegaard would have admired at this point.

The terms 'paradox' and 'absurd', then, must be thought of in either an existential or a behavioral sense, but not a logical sense. Kierkegaard was himself a masterly logical theorist. It is a gross misinterpretation to accuse him of advocating logical paradoxicality, absurdity, or the rejection of reason.

5. Kierkegaard "exalts 'the knights of faith' above the moral law; he believes in a 'teleological suspension' of ethics."

Prof. Paton is guilty of an error common to many interpreters of Kierkegaard, namely, the failure to take account of the pseudonymous authorship of many of Kierkegaard's (primarily earlier) works. The above-mentioned views concerning the knights of faith and the teleological suspension of the ethical are found in the work, *Fear and Trembling*. But, strictly speaking, the author of the work is not Kierkegaard, but Johannes de Silentio, an imaginary author purposely created by Kierkegaard for the task of expressing these views.[22] Any opinions expressed by this pseudonymous author, or any of the other pseudonyms, must not be identified with the final position which Kierkegaard himself defended.[23]

In the case of *Fear and Trembling*, the author (pseudonymous author) is clearly an aesthete, but he is interested in the figure of Abraham: how the latter is the author of faith. He enjoys toying with Abraham as the first knight of faith. The pseudonymous author makes no pretensions of being a man of faith himself. In this work, it is the author-aesthete who speaks, not Kierkegaard. It is thus entirely inappropriate to attribute the views of the pseudonymous author to Kierkegaard.

A further comment. Even if Kierkegaard had maintained the exaltation of the knights of faith and believed in a teleological suspension of the ethical, is this a fact which deserves condemnation? For the insights which Kierkegaard's author develops are worthy of serious consideration, and ought not to be as hastily dismissed as they are by Prof. Paton. Let us consider this matter with respect to one of the issues raised in the book, the teleological suspension of the ethical.[24]

The problem is posed in this way. Is there any such thing as a teleological suspension of the ethical, that is, a purposeful suspension of the ethical? We all suspend the ethical non-teleologically. But does the religious mode of existence sometimes require that the ethical be intentionally suspended? If so, then there arises a conflict between the ethical and the religious.

The point made by Kierkegaard's author is that religion may involve a departure from the universal ethical norm. He suggests that God may be incommensurate, outside the norm. This is what Abraham dared to assert. The individual, when under a divine com-

---

[22] The title page of this work reads:
    Fear and Trembling
    A dialectical Lyric
    by Johannes de Silentio
    Copenhagen, 1843

[23] See, e.g., Paul L. Holmer, "Kierkegaard and Ethical Theory." *Ethics*, Vol. LXIII, No. 3, April, 1953, p. 159.
Whereas the pseudonymous works do not express Kierkegaard's own views, the religious writings (comprising a majority of his volumes) do. Certain works (*Fragments* and *Postscript*, e.g.) are intermediary and express Kierkegaard's more philosophical doctrines. This body of literature, of varying types, is not understood unless one also reads Kierkegaard's literature about the literature. For the latter, see *The Point of View*, transl. by W. Lowrie (London, Oxford: 1939); the Journals; and "A First and Last Declaration" (appended to the *Postscript*).

[24] *Fear and Trembling*, Problem 1, pp. 79ff.

mand, is higher than the universal. He sees that God is not wholly commensurate with the universal norm, that he may not be described or describable by the universal standards of an ethical society. Thus, an individual may, at times, have to suspend the ethical, teleologically, with intent, in order fully to obey what he takes to be the divine command.

Perhaps there is a certain insight here which merits our attention. Unless one makes a complete identification of the religious and the ethical, then there is no reason for assuming that the ethical may not be required to be purposefully suspended on occasion. We acknowledge this to some extent in our Western society. The case of the conscientious objector is a good example. But even if one desired no association with the religious, one might nonetheless make a good case for the desirability of maintaining the possibility of teleologically suspending the ethical. One can, say, be a conscientious objector even though one is not a religious man. All this is merely to point out that a cavalier dismissal of the doctrine of the teleological suspension of the ethical, or any other issue, is to be avoided.

6. "We should be particularly on our guard when the guide (Kierkegaard) makes no pretence at objective thinking, which stands or falls by the argument independently of the personality of the thinker, but rests his case on the inwardness of his own personal experience."

This assertion is commonly made about Kierkegaard. It is clearly false. One of the most impressive features of Kierkegaard's writings is the remarkable philosophical detachment with which he wrote. A high degree of disinterestedness pervades his writings and displays the objectivity which he could practice even on matters which have a highly subjective and personal concern. In the domain of knowledge, disinterestedness and objectivity are necessary. Kierkegaard admitted this, and himself displayed the required neutrality. He is an extremely rational and logical thinker.

This is not to deny that there are poetical and persuasive features about his writings. Many commentators have centered their attention upon these features and have neglected the logical structure of the literature. But anyone who carefully reads the *Fragments* and *Postscript*, for example, will be impressed with the high degree of objectivity which Kierkegaard commands with respect to the various problems which come up for consideration, some of which are in themselves non-objective, yet are treated in a detached manner.

It is unfortunate that few critics have noted the detached philo-

sophical ability with which Kierkegaard wrote and the neutral dialecti-
cal structure which he exhibits as a thinker. For even his discussion
of the realm of interests, passions, and concerns is generally performed
in a disinterested manner. And although his *life* was centered around
a controlling passion, the Christian faith, his works are restrained by an
intellectual dialectic, a neutral, regulated, and structured thought.

For example, Kierkegaard believed that to a disinterested and
dispassionate knower there were always genuine existential alternatives – various modes of existence which were possibilities to be actualized. He distinguishes at least four of these: the aesthetic, the ethical,
Religion A, and Religion B. Intelligence could guarantee no supremacy
for any *one* of these. Reflection, rather, always reveals a *plurality* of
possible ethical modes. All four can, thus, be portrayed – and are so
portrayed by Kierkegaard – with equal plausibility. One can always
find valid reasons for all four, if one surveyed them objectively. And
this is precisely what Kierkegaard did. His consideration of all of them
is controlled by a logical, neutral structure. (And he never suggests
that intelligence would lead one to affirm the Christian alternative
as the *true* one).

Thus Prof. Paton's charge that Kierkegaard "makes no pretence
at objective thinking, which stands or falls by the argument independently of the thinker, but rests his case on the inwardness of his
own personal experience" is false with respect to Kierkegaard as a
thinker. That Kierkegaard resolves his personal decision of faith and
existence in inwardness is another matter. For *here* one is speaking of
Kierkegaard, not as a thinker, but as an existing man. That is, Kierkegaard's choice of the Christian mode of existence as the one for him
to actualize was certainly a matter of subjective concern. But then,
on what basis does one select one alternative, rather than another?
Because one is more rational than another? Kierkegaard says, No.
For, as I have said, Kierkegaard's objectivity allowed him to give
equal rational plausibility to *all* the possible (major) modes of existence.
The embracing of *one* alternative, however, is an existential leap, based
on one's passions and concerns. This is simply to say that there is a
difference between knowing what a mode of existence is and living it.

But I shall refrain from commenting further on this point. For
Prof. Paton's criticism had to do with Kierkegaard as a thinker, and
not as an existing man. As a thinker, Kierkegaard was intellectually
neutral. He writes objectively and detachedly about subjectivity and
interests. He insists that all discourse about subjectivity and passion

(including his own) be submitted to the same logical scrutiny and analysis which characterizes discourse on more objective matters.

7. "If ever a person was self-centered it was Kierkegaard: he hardly
ever thinks of anyone but himself. Self-centeredness is the very
antithesis of religion."

It is true that Kierkegaard was intensely concerned about his own
existence. Thus Prof. Paton's concluding charge is more nearly
justified than the preceding ones were. But to say that Kierkegaard
"hardly thinks of anyone but himself" is not true. His concern about
others may be seen by reading *The Works of Love*. His concern for God
(even though knowledge of his existence was objectively uncertain)
may be seen in his religious writings and prayers. Hence, this charge,
although it has been made by many writers, particularly religious
critics,[25] is a superficial one at this level. Here the works of Kierkegaard speak with greater accuracy than the commentaries do.

More serious is the assertion that Kierkegaard ought not to have
been self-centered (to the degree in which he was), as self-centeredness
is "the very antithesis to religion." Kierkegaard himself gave the most
satisfactory answer to this criticism. In *The Works of Love* he states
the manner in which Christianity presupposes self-love.[26] By this,
Kierkegaard does not recommend total self-centeredness, with utter
disregard for all others. The remainder of the book refutes that charge.
What Kierkegaard means is: Each individual must at least love
himself to a sufficient degree that he is concerned about his own
destiny, or, in the case of the religious man, about his eternal happiness.

Kierkegaard holds that a supposed lack of interest in one's self is a
deviation from the norm. After all, the Christian ethical command is
to love one's neighbour *as one's self*. This implies that the self is to be
loved, in at least a minimal sense, and not merely negated. Now the
Christian religion may be wrong. However, if one accepts the Christian
view, then certainly Kierkegaard is correct with respect to what such
acceptance implies about a concern for one's self.

Furthermore, Kierkegaard, while emphasizing the need for disinterestedness and objectivity with respect to knowledge, finds a
detached attitude in the ethico-religious realm (or in existence in
general) to be despicable. Here there must be a maximization of
personal concern and interestedness. Part of this concern must be for
one's self, unless one professes to be something less than a man, perhaps

25 E.g., H. R. Niebuhr, *Christ and Culture*, chap. 7.
26 S. Kierkegaard, *The Works of Love* (Princeton: Princeton Press) p. 15.

after the fashion of the speculative philosopher, who seeks to appropriate everything into universal categories – even ex istence!

II

I have tried to show that Prof. Paton's interpretation of Kierkegaard is a distorted and at least partly falsified one. To be sure, at a rather superficial level, nearly every one of his assertions is true. However, with further explication, we may see that gross misinterpretations are conveyed by Prof. Paton's bold but naïve comments on Kierkegaard's views. His judgments concerning Kierkegaard are as cursory and inadequate as mine would be concerning Kant if I were to say that Kant believes that metaphysics is impossible, and gave no explication of my statement. Kant's philosophy demands more than such cryptic, superficial attacks. And so does Kierkegaard's.

Furthermore, I wish to emphasize that the misinterpretations which I have discussed are not peculiar to Prof. Paton. They are extremely widespread, particularly those concerning Kierkegaard's alleged irrationality, illogicality, and lack of objectivity. I hope that I have at least made a start towards clarifying some of the issues about which there has been much confusion. In so doing, I should not wish to give the impression that I hold the Danish author to be beyond criticism, or that I slavishly align myself with his views. On the contrary, I believe that several of Kierkegaard's views can be justifiably criticized, and that others allow alternative stances. But this is not the place at which I can elaborate this point. All I have tried to do here is to shed light upon some rather persistent confusions and misinterpretations.

It must be admitted that Kierkegaard's writings lend themselves rather readily to misinterpretation. The device of the pseudonyms, the special meanings attached to words which have other connotations, the abstract terminology in some passages, the highly imaginative nature of other passages, the mingling of jest and seriousness – all these perhaps account for the fact that Kierkegaard is a difficult author to understand and is therefore apt to be misinterpreted unless the reader has a familiarity with the entire literature and a sufficient background to be able to understand the technical problems posed by many of the writings. Thus, perhaps the use of commentaries is to be recommended. But, alas, while there are many works which discuss certain features of Kierkegaard's writings (some of which even attempt to compile a Kierkegaardian system!) there are not many which accurately convey the central problems which the writings present.[27] The works of Kierkegaard still await their definitive interpreter.

---

[27] I find the analyses of David Swenson and Paul L. Holmer to be more reliable than most of the literature about Kierkegaard which exists today.

CHAPTER II

KIERKEGAARD, LOGICALITY AND THE CHRISTIAN FAITH

It has become common to think of Søren Kierkegaard as being an irrationalist. Both those who are in opposition to Kierkegaard's thought and those who count themselves as allies have made use of him in this fashion. After spending years in studying the works of Kierkegaard, I have come to believe that his views have been grossly distorted and misinterpreted by the readers of both sides. The following remarks are in the way of prolegomena to this subject and attempt to clarify some of the confusion which has been disseminated in the past years.

I

Can Christianity or the Hebrew-Christian heritage be viewed from a logical standpoint? Are Christianity and Judaism criticizable? Can we impose upon the Hebrew-Christian tradition the categories of reason? Paul Minear, Émile Cailliet, Karl Barth, and J. Haroutunian say No to all these questions. Kierkegaard announces a decisive Yes to all of them – which may be rather surprising to many people, since Kierkegaard is usually portrayed as being a kind of arch-irrationalist. What accounts for this difference in thought? And how does Kierkegaard differ from the above-mentioned group on this matter of logicality? This is the subject to be explored in these pages.

Minear, Cailliet, Barth, and Haroutunian are four representative thinkers of the view which holds that Christianity and Judaism cannot be viewed from a rational standpoint (at least, without performing a great injustice). The Hebrew-Christian tradition is anti-Greek, anti-rational, or supra-rational, they say. We cannot impose the categories of reason on it. There exists a capacity in men, the eyes of faith, which is different from the eyes of reason. Thus Christianity is not externally or neutrally criticizable. There is no point on the outside from which we can rationally view Christianity or Judaism; no point from which we can understand them in a logical sense.

The history of the Bible, according to Barth, one of the champions of this view, is different from all other histories.[1] The forms and moods of apprehension are different from ours. There is "a profound discontinuity between the Bible and any other book not dependent upon it, between the mind of the Bible (sic) and any 'natural' mind, between the soul of the Hebrews and the soul of others," says Haroutunian.[2] There is an "inner and intrinsic otherness of the prophetic view," says the biblical scholar, Paul Minear.[3] "The eyes of faith enable us to see things differently from the eyes of unbelief."[4] "The Western mind insists on forcing the Semitic imagination into the straitjacket of its own conceptual logic ... 'No Semite is afraid of a logical contradiction.' "[5] The modern philosopher poses questions in a form "alien to the outlook of prophets and apostles."[6] "When man seeks to share his store of conceptual knowledge," he uses such forms as "careful philosophical definition; precise, prosaic propositions; logical syllogism ... But these forms of discourse are conspicuous by their rarity in Scripture. Is not this scarcity due in part to the fact that these forms seldom succeed in producing non-accumulative knowledge or in precipitating existential consciousness?"[7]

Émile Cailliet agrees with Barth, Haroutunian, and Minear, and attempts to support this view in a consideration of logic, with evidence cited from his studies in anthropology under Lévy-Bruhl. The presupposition that human logic is always everywhere the same is groundless, says Cailliet. "The ways of thinking of primitive man are undeniably shot through with uncanny forms of logic – a confused logic – to us misinformed and often obscure ... The primitive world has a unity of its own. The various activities of the natives seem coherent when viewed from within."[8] We note breaks of continuity in the primitive mentality, as if the process of thought had been interrupted by "a sudden, puzzling inspiration." The logic of such a mind-set "treads

---

[1] Karl Barth, *The Word of God and the Word of Man* (Chicago: Pilgrim Press, 1928), chap. ii.

[2] J. Haroutunian, *Religion in Life*, XII (Summer, 1943), p. 382.

[3] Paul Minear, *The Eyes of Faith* (Philadelphia: Westminster Press, 1946), p. 5.

[4] *Ibid.*, pp. 6, 7.

[5] *Ibid.*, p. 24.

[6] *Ibid.*

[7] *Ibid.*, p. 170.

[8] É. Cailliet, "Frontiers of Logic." *Theology Today*, VI (1950), 465ff.

paths not familiar to our own."[9] We must thus distinguish between a "primitive" attitude or mentality and a "civilized" one. In the former we see a type of mind "which has not yet disentangled itself from the reality in which the group is submerged."[10] The Bible takes for granted this relativity of our human logic and manifests a different logic or mind-set from that of, say, the Greeks.

The view shared by these four thinkers denies that there is a neutral, logical standpoint from which one can view Christianity or the Hebrew-Christian tradition. In effect, only men of faith can understand Christianity or Judaism. Furthermore, the Hebrew-Christian tradition is not subject to the categories of logic. The tools of philosophical precision are inappropriate for understanding this tradition, since the latter contains logical paradoxicality, a fact which is accounted for by the peculiar mind-set of the biblical age.

Kierkegaard opposes this view. For him there exists a logical, rational standpoint on the outside, from which one can view Christianity and understand it in a logical sense. "It is ... possible to consider objectively what Christianity is, in that the inquirer sets this question objectively before him, leaving aside for the present the question of its truth (the truth is subjectivity)."[11] Kierkegaard continues: "The possibility of knowing what Christianity is without being a Christian must therefore be affirmed."[12]

Before elaborating upon this, I should like to refer to the view of W. F. Albright, a scholar of Semitic languages, archaeology, and Hebrew history and religion, which opposes that of Cailliet with respect to the Hebrew-Christian tradition and its supposed lack of logicality.

Empirical logic (e.g., Proverbs) achieved a signal triumph in the Old Testament where survivals from the age of pre-logical thinking are very few and far between. With it man reached a point where his best judgments about his relation to God, his fellow men, and the world, were in most respects not appreciably inferior to ours. In fundamental ethical and spiritual matters, we have not progressed at all beyond the empirico-logical world of the Old Testament, or the unrivaled combination of prelogical intuition, empiricological wisdom, and logical deduction which we find in the New Testament. In fact, a very large section of modern religion, literature, and art actually represents a pronounced retrogression when compared with the Old Testament.[13]

[9] *Ibid.*, p. 472.

[10] *Ibid.*, pp. 474–75.

[11] Søren Kierkegaard. *Concluding Unscientific Postscript* (Princeton: Princeton University Press, 1941), p. 331.

[12] *Ibid.*, p. 332.

[13] W. F. Albright, *Archeology and the Religion of Israel* (Baltimore: Johns Hopkins Press, 1953), p. 33.

If we accept the views of Minear and others, we are faced with the impossibility of considering Christianity and Judaism from a logical standpoint. I believe that the statement by Albright concerning the invalidity of this position historically and the view of Kierkegaard concerning the present necessity of opposing this sublogical or supralogical view are worth considering. I know of no one who has spoken so decisively on the issue as Kierkegaard. That Kierkegaard is a first-rate logician and a kind of precursor of the contemporary concern for language and clarification may be seen by a careful scrutiny of his works. However, this is an aspect of him which Barth, Brunner, Minear, and others simply have not noted in their use of him.

The following discussion is merely an effort to state what Kierkegaard, in fact, said. I shall not here criticize his views. This does not mean that I am in agreement with them.

II

We might begin with the meaning of 'paradox' in Kierkegaard. It is important to note at the outset a meaning of 'paradox' which is *not* found in Kierkegaard's writings when he talks about paradoxicality. This is the logical paradox. In, e.g., the diagram called the "square of opposition" by traditional logicians, A and O are contradictories, as are I and E. A logical paradox is the kind of sentence which asserts that opposites, such as A and O, are both true or both false. The logician says that a paradox of this sort is impossible to reflect on. If A is true, O must be false, and vice versa. Unreflecting Christians have sometimes involved themselves in matters of logical paradoxes. They have failed to see that they should not have identified paradoxicality with alogicality or contradictoriness. Others, who have stressed the need for logic and have feared paradoxes, have failed to distinguish, as seen below, logical paradoxes from behavioral ones.

Kierkegaard did not fall into this error of committing or advocating logical paradoxes. He distinguishes a behavioral paradox from a logical paradox.[14] He gives no indication that Christianity involves a person in logical paradoxicality. Indeed, he attacks this type of sloppy thinking. Paradox in Kierkegaard's literature is existential rather than logical. Christ as the Absolute Paradox in his writings is not

---

[14] *Philosophical Fragments* (Princeton: Princeton University Press, 1938), chap. iii; *Postscript*, p. 196.

Christ as the logical contradictory. For one cannot violate the rules of logic and make sense. Kierkegaard is insistent upon this point. It is difficult to see how religious people have made him an advocate of logical paradoxicality.

The paradox of Christianity (and this is the paradox Kierkegaard stresses) is a paradoxicality of interests and values.[15] We may best illustrate this by following Kierkegaard's procedure. He refers to the Greek tradition throughout the *Philosophical Fragments*, which assumed man as the measure of all things.[16] It stressed an analogy between the known and the unknown.[17] To make an inference about the unknown, in Greek thought, you do so by analogy with the known. Thus God must be like the known. His qualities were held to be commensurate with those of men. The Greeks posited incommensurateness only in the negative sense of evil and the demonic.

But Christians have pursued this same method of making God commensurate with the main values of life. They have often defined the principal ends and values of life to be wealth, health, long life, pleasure, happiness, usefulness, security, peace, etc. This is the sense in which Kierkegaard uses the term 'reason' when he refers to the paradox. The above values are "reasonable" expectations to most people. Needless to say, this sense of 'reason' differs from rationality in the strict sense.

Now most people like to believe that God is somehow commensurate with all the above-mentioned values. But the question of importance is, as Kierkegaard sees it: Is God on the same level with these values? According to New Testament Christianity, Christ does not necessarily increase one's comfort, pleasure, etc. Here is the paradoxicality of Christianity, says Kierkegaard. It is *not* a paradoxicality which violates the fundamental principles of reason. It is the "paradox" of having one's ordinary sense of interests and values disturbed by meeting God in Christ. This creates an opposition (a behavioral opposition, not a logical one). And, because of it, one may acquire a new set of values if one's life is sufficiently disturbed. For Kierkegaard, one cannot add God in Christ to the pattern of values already existing. This would be paganism. He seems to have the New Testament behind him on this point. Men then and now have followed

---

[15] *Fragments*, p. 37.
[16] *Ibid.*, p. 30.
[17] *Ibid.*, p. 36.

Christ even though it meant an unreasonable demand – giving up all, suffering for Christ, dying to the world, etc.

III

A second factor which needs to be emphasized is the fact that there are alternative systems of values which confront every individual.[18] Kierkegaard describes several of these in the *Stages*. No one of the alternative systems of values can any longer claim to be the only rational one, while all the others are irrational.[19] There can be no *one* ultimate rational ground other than logicality itself, and the latter does not solve problems of existence. For example, the existence of God cannot be asserted on rational grounds as being the only rational alternative between existence or non-existence (of God). "There is too much in the world to prevent this," one might say, equally well with: "There is much in nature to affirm his existence." Both the theistic position and the non-theistic position can be rationally stated, each as an organized view. One cannot say that one is rational while the other is not. Kierkegaard makes this clear in the notion of the Stages, in which he posits four views of life: the aesthetic, the ethical, religion A (general religiosity), and religion B (Christianity). (Of course, one can add others too.) No one of the views is more rationally defensible than the others. The argument frequently made by Christians and others has been that one of the four is *the* rational way of life. They are all rationally defensible, says Kierkegaard. It is when we come to the matter of existence that the trouble begins.[20]

For example, one view of life says that the highest good is pleasure. But another view is that the highest good is duty. From a rational, logical standpoint, either is in itself defensible. It is when I note concretely in existence what it means to pursue the pleasure way of life that I find that I cannot *maximally* pursue both pleasure and duty *at once*. (In a minimal pursuit, there can be overlapping, of course.) When attempting to act, I cannot realize both views. There are unresolvable behavioral differences. Now the attempt is sometimes made to translate the problem from the behavioral level to the in-

---

[18] D. Swenson, *Something About Kierkegaard* (Minneapolis: Augsburg Press, 1941) p. 117; Paul Holmer, "Kierkegaard and Ethical Theory."

[19] *Postscript*, p. 262.

[20] *Ibid.*, pp. 285ff.

tellectual level by asking: Which one of them is *true*? But this achieves no results. One has merely transferred the behavioral skepticism to a new level, that of intelligence. And intelligence solves no problems of behavior – that is, behavioral decisions are primarily based on subrational factors. Intelligence functions only in ideality or possibility, portraying and giving content to the various alternatives which confront one. Intelligence never functions in reality or actuality.[21] Intelligence may function in delineating the alternatives or in perhaps rationalizing a choice after one has acted. But the performance of an action is an existential accomplishment, not an intellectual one.

Kierkegaard holds that, from the point of view of an objective, detached, disinterested intelligence, one can get at least four major alternatives. From this intelligent, logical standpoint, one can describe each of the four (and any others) accurately. Each has something to say on all or most of the major issues of life. Many religious people do not realize this and consider the other views to be intellectually inferior. The Christian view is superior, they say, because it more adequately explains the origin of things, etc. But if this were so, the atheist would have been convinced long ago. But atheists from Lucretius to Bertrand Russell have needed neither religion nor God to explain things. Therefore, one cannot justifiably call the atheist irrational. Both the theistic view and the atheistic view may be rational.

What, then, determines the adequacy – I do not say logical cogency – of one view over the other? Not intelligence and argumentation, but *interestedness*. It is the disposition provided by one's convictions and interests that explains the differences among men – some of them affirming a religious view and some a non-religious view. The adequacy of one over the other is a function of one's interest, passion, subjectivity, and concern. This is why some men find one view to be superior and others adhere to different views. But to affirm and actualize a view of life upon the basis of these subjective factors is far from being logical, which means a capacity for disinterested objectivity, for being able to examine an idea without being committed to it, a capacity which does not diminish the number of alternatives which confront it by attempting to prove one to be rational and the others to be irrational.[22]

Kierkegaard, then, proposes that men as reasonable creatures can

---

[21] *Ibid.*, pp. 279ff.
[22] Holmer, *op. cit.*, p. 159.

disinterestedly look at the alternative views of life (or any other subject) and understand them all, including Christianity, in a logical manner.[23] The eyes of faith are not needed for this purpose. Our neutral, logical standpoint is sufficient for providing content to all the views of life, including Christianity.[24]

Kierkegaard insists that this fact be not overlooked. The case for there being a logical standpoint implies that Christianity can be stated, discussed, and understood without one's being a Christian[25] and that our instruments of thought are sufficiently neutral to be able to describe any conceivable content – Christian as well as non-Christian. The view of Minear, Cailliet, Haroutunian, Barth, etc., leads to the notion that neutral humans cannot understand Christianity – or Judaism – and that our instruments of thought are not neutral. Kierkegaard holds to the possibility of objectivity here, which means a neutral state in which the maximum of understanding can take place. Christianity can be surveyed from such a neutral, logical standpoint. Kierkegaard demonstrated the validity of this proposition by himself discussing Christianity with a remarkable detachment in many of his works.

IV

The denial of a logical standpoint from which to view alternatives accounts for much of biblical scholarship. Some have said that the difficulty in belief for many people is due to the fact of living in a later generation, far from the initial thrust of the gospel in the lifetime of Jesus Christ. If we go back to the first generation, it is said, the difficulty disappears. Thus the mad rush of textual studies, etc., ensues. The first generation of believers had an advantage, it is held. Contemporaneity in time is a condition for understanding. Scholarship must try to recover it.

Kierkegaard points out that this is not so.[26] And it ought to be quite obvious. The first generation had in it a few who believed (to the end) and many who did not believe. There was not unanimity then and variety now. There was diversity then too. In the first generation

[23] *Postscript*, chap. iii.
[24] Holmer, *op. cit.*, p. 162.
[25] *Postscript*, p. 332.
[26] *Fragments*, chaps. iv–v.

there occurred not only the adoration of Christ but the crucifixion too. It was logically possible to be an unbeliever in the first generation, just as it is now. The only difference is that in the time of Jesus' historical existence, the proclamation of the gospel was news of the day, while for subsequent generations it is a matter of scholarship.[27] But neither one of news of the day nor scholarship is more certain than the other. Both lead only to claiming the historical existence of Jesus, in some form as the following: "There was a man, Jesus, who lived ..." Neither leads to the significantly religious proposition that Jesus was God or the Son of God or divine which has a lot to do with Christianity. Just as it is not absolutely clear to us that he was divine, so it was not clear to the first generation. Many called him a base deceiver.

Some would insist that, by hearing Jesus' voice, by seeing his loving kindness, and perhaps witnessing his miracles, etc., they would have an advantage and thereby see that Jesus is divine. But if this is so, how is the crucifixion to be explained? People could not infer from what was visible that Jesus was necessarily divine. All that the news of the day could say was that Jesus existed. This is all that scholarship can assert. It cannot deal with the meaning of faith for individual men today. Scholarship can never give you the truth for you.[28]

But then in what sort of way does the affirmation that Jesus is God and man have meaning? This is not a *meaningful* proposition, says Kierkegaard throughout the *Postscript*, preceding the logical empiricists in this observation and distinction between meaningful and non-meaningful sentences by nearly a century. That is, the assertion is non-cognitive. It is, rather, the kind of expression that has significance only when one lives a new kind of *life*. Its significance has to do with the passional life of the man who utters it. It is not significant in the cognitive sense of stating an objective truth which can be verified.

Now one can delineate the content of this assertion and of others which make up the central statements about Christianity, from the outside, without assenting to the content. This is what we mean by a logical standpoint. But thought does not reduce the alternatives. It only systematically delineates them. One still has equality among the alternatives after thought. Thought does not decide what you should *be*, which view of life you should embrace and actualize.[29]

What does reduce the alternatives? We have already answered

[27] *Ibid.*, pp. 46f.
[28] *Ibid.*, p. 71.
[29] Holmer, *op. cit.*, pp. 162–63.

this. It is interestedness, passion. The distinction between being aesthetic, ethical, religious, or Christian can be resolved not by rational reflection but by passion, care, concern, and despair. Reflection can state the differences and put them in a communicable form. It allows one to state the problem for thought but not to solve it behaviorally. The latter depends upon where one has his interest.[30]

In the case of Christianity, the question may be asked: How does one acquire the degree of interestedness by which he embraces the Christian view? The answer according to Kierkegaard is: By removing all the impediments – illusory securities, false gods, inadequate goals – that keep one from centering his life on Jesus Christ and therefore by enabling men to come to the point of redemption as a last resort, when other things no longer can safeguard them.[31] If the despair in such a crisis is deep enough, this may be the nexus between the self and any one of the four alternatives. Christianity presupposes a maximization of despair.[32] When there is nothing else to believe in and one feels himself sinful, he may satisfy the condition in which he can make a behavioral leap – Christian or otherwise.

We ought now to be able to understand better the nature of paradoxicality in Christianity. The paradox is rooted in what Kierkegaard calls the "unhappy relation" between my organized system of values and the demand of Christianity.[33] To the degree that I become interested in the Christian appeal, I may have to give up all. Jesus Christ is not added to my normal values and ends. For me to be a Christian, says Kierkegaard, may mean that I will have to give up all interests and goals in order to follow Christ. Thus no one is a Christian by first birth. One must become an unconditional believer, whereby he is willing to give up all personal conditions and preferences.[34] Then the behavioral paradoxicality disappears, not permanently, but in moments and hours, as life keeps fluctuating.[35]

And faith, Kierkegaard says, is the "happy relation" between my organized self and the paradox.[36] It is the state in which my interests coincide with the demand of Christianity. Again, it must be pointed out that faith is not belief. Faith is non-noetic. It is more akin to an

---

[30] *Postscript*, pp. 117, 282.
[31] *Ibid.*, p. 375.
[32] Swenson, *op. cit.*, p. 111.
[33] *Fragments*, p. 39.
[34] Kierkegaard, *The Point of View* (London: Oxford University Press, 1939), pp. 159–60.
[35] *Postscript*, p. 75.
[36] *Fragments*, p. 47.

embracing which involves the whole self, not merely the logical faculties, but one's entire being.

It should be clear that to ask whether the act of giving up all to follow Christ is better or truer than any other view of life cannot be answered. For the one who makes the leap to embrace Christianity does so in virtue of his despairing, not in virtue of objective certainty. This act of faith never weights the matter in an objective sense and never shows that all the other views are false. In other words, as has been already mentioned, faith is non-noetic.[37] It does not bring knowledge, or a higher degree of *objective* certainty. Further, faith, Kierkegaard says, is not immediacy.[38] Or sometimes he calls it "immediacy after reflection," not before reflection.[39] Immediacy before reflection is sensory experience of God.[40] Kierkegaard calls this "paganism." Christianity posits immediacy of an ethical, behavioral sort after reflection. Faith occurs after doubt and despair.[41] This is why Christianity presupposes a second birth,[42] a man's highest transformation of himself, which is his ultimate truth.[43]

V

We have reached the crux of the matter now. Christianity is both a view of existing and a way of existing, says Kierkegaard. To grasp Christianity as a view of existing only is to understand Christianity, but it is not to become a Christian. We may now complete an earlier quotation of Kierkegaard. The first part of the statement reads: "The possibility of knowing what Christianity is without being a Christian must therefore be affirmed." Kierkegaard goes on to say – and this is the important point which Minear, Cailliet, etc., overlook – "It is a different question whether a man can know what it is to be a Christian without being one, which must be denied."[44] "There is a tremendous difference between knowing what Christianity is and being a Christian."[45]

[37] *Ibid.*, p. 50; *Postscript*, p. 30.
[38] *Postscript*, p. 310.
[39] *Ibid.*, pp. 102, xix; *Fragments*, p. 70; see also *The Point of View*, pp. 68–69.
[40] *Fragments*, p. 71.
[41] *Postscript*, p. 218.
[42] *Fragments*, p. 13.
[43] *Postscript*, p. 38.
[44] *Ibid.*, p. 332.
[45] *Ibid.*, p. 339.

To grasp Christianity as a way of existing is to become a Christian. The only persons who need Christianity as a view of existing are those who have a reflective bent to their personalities.[46] But we should not negate this factor. One who is intelligent should utilize his intelligence and have a view. It would be an imperfection for him not to do so.[47] Christianity can thus be logically conceived before being realized. Therefore, it can be talked about and preached. And this does not falsify as to what Christianity is. But, according to Kierkegaard, the perfection of the Christian life does not come when one understands what is said. It is realized only when one makes it *actual* in a new birth.[48]

Man, then, is faced by various alternative possibilities.[49] Christian faith is the actualizing of one of them. When a person embraces one of the alternatives by transforming it from a possibility to a concrete actuality in his life, this is an act of faith.[50] This act of faith is not a matter of truth or ignorance, but a resolution of despair and of doubt.[51] When all the alternative views of life are placed before one, one is asked to choose. The act of choosing – and this is the leap – is faith.[52] Again faith is shown to be non-cognitive. Rather it is behavioral and existential.

What keeps men from faithing? (I use 'faithing' rather than 'believing' to distinguish the non-cognitive from the cognitive function.) Kierkegaard has done much to trace this to the lack of a need for faithing, which is hidden from people because of the illusions which cover the need.[53] When the illusions in which people place their faith are destroyed, *faith* results and drives men to God. In his view, one of the central tasks of Christianity, then, is to take away illusions from people so that the need for faith may arise.[54] As long as men live under these illusions or believe that they can live self-contained lives, God does not exist for them Or, as a Kierkegaard scholar has stated the issue: "A self-annihilation of the individual before God is man's truth and his highest perfection as a human being."[55]

---

[46] *Ibid.*, p. 331.
[47] *Ibid.*, pp. 311–12.
[48] See Kierkegaard, *Purity of Heart* (New York: Harper & Bros., 1938).
[49] *Postscript*, p. 320.
[50] *Ibid.*, pp. 302, 306.
[51] *Fragments*, p. 69.
[52] *Postscript*, p. 91.
[53] *Ibid.*, p. 374.
[54] *Point of View*, pp. 34, 40.
[55] Swenson *op. cit.*, p. 127.

CHAPTER III

KIERKEGAARD'S ETHICAL THEORY

I would like to discuss primarily two issues in this chapter. The first has to do with what I take to be Kierkegaard's views *about* ethical theory – the question, roughly, as to whether a science of ethics is possible. The second deals with a more specific issue *within* ethics – the question as to whether intersubjectively valid ethical judgments are possible. The two are closely related. Indeed, the second is perhaps a more specific formulation of the first. The method of approaching each will differ, however.

The interpreter of Kierkegaard faces a problem in connection with the first of these issues – Kierkegaard's views on ethical theory. The problem arises from the fact that Kierkegaard nowhere fully *states* his theory about ethical theory. He, rather, for the most part, demonstrates it and allows the reader to develop the exposition of it. Thus, in my discussion of the first issue, I am not always able to cite specific *passages* by which to support my statements. I can only recommend that the reader study Kierkegaard's "aesthetic" writings plus some of the religious works. I believe that if he has done so, he will find my exposition to make explicit what is implicit in Kierkegaard's works. On certain points there is ambiguity in the Kierkegaardian literature. I might say, however, that my discussion is, in large measure, compatible with the views of two capable Kierkegaard scholars – David Swenson and Paul L. Holmer.[1]

The second issue which I shall discuss – whether or not intersubjectively valid ethical judgments are possible – does not involve the problem of the lack of explicit textual statements. On the contrary,

---

[1] David F. Swenson, *Something About Kierkegaard*. (Mpls: Augsburg: 1941) *passim*. Paul L. Holmer, "Kierkegaard and Ethical Theory," *Ethics*, Vol. LXIII, No. 3, April 1953, pp. 157–170. I am especially indebted to Professor Holmer in the first section of this paper.

Kierkegaard deals with the issue at great length.[2] However, another problem arises here. Kierkegaard's discussion of the issue is an extremely difficult one. Perhaps this is why most commentators have avoided the subject. After considerable effort, I hope to be able to explicate Kierkegaard's views on the problem.

In a third section, I shall, briefly, comment upon Kierkegaard's views on the two problems, indicating how one might attempt to support the views of the Danish author.

I

Kierkegaard's theory about ethical theory is expressed through his doctrine of the Stages. As I mentioned, the theory is not merely stated or expounded in his literature. It is portrayed. The portrayal was accomplished by means of the device of using pseudonyms – invented authors who structuralize various modes of existence. Each of the invented authors expresses his likes and dislikes, concerns, interests, and theories. Each is construed "ideally," that is, in the form of a normative type, rather than after the fashion of most existing men, who are often complex and multiple personalities. Each invented author, then, develops in a literary and reflective form the ideal proportions and characteristics of one mode of existence. These are so delineated that several distinctively different modes result. Four of these stand out: the aesthetic, the ethical, Religion A, and Religion B (Christianity).

What is the philosophical purpose underlying this literary kind of presentation? It is to show that to a disinterested and cognizing subject there are always genuine ethical *alternatives*. Reflection does not reduce the multiplicity to a unity. Rather, it increases the plausibility of each of the various multiples. A scientific or philosophical ethics – in the sense of a discipline which can resolve ultimate differences concerning the good, etc. – is hence, a chimera. *All* of the various modes of existence, that is, all of the alternative answers to the questions 'What is the good?', 'What ought I to do?', etc., can be given equal rational plausibility to the genuinely reflective man. Intelligence can give no "higher" plausibility to any one of the various modes.

[2] S. Kierkegaard, *Concluding Unscientific Postscript*. Tr. by Walter Lowrie and David F. Swenson (Princeton: Princeton University Press, 1941) pp. 267ff.

Thus, since a neutral, disinterested intelligence can never solve the problem of the multiplicity of alternatives, since it can never decide objectively that *this* mode of existence is the right one whereas others are wrong, no science of ethics is possible. To a disinterested knowing subject, there is no single good. There are, similarly, no *rational* or logical grounds for any ethical choice. Rather, the more one's intelligence is maximized, the more one finds that there are only *numerous* possible modes of existence, each of which remains as a genuine and valid alternative. For such maximization of intelligence gives better reasons for *all* of the alternative possibles.

Kierkegaard, thus, writes in opposition to such thinkers as Hegel, e.g., who thought that the multiplicity of alternatives could be reduced to a unity by means of a more enlightened reflection. Kierkegaard suggests that all such theories are inadequate, as they do violence to the facts which confront one who reflects on this matter. As I have said, intelligence does not merely discover alternatives; it gives greater credence to *each* of them. Hence, one is always left in objective uncertainty in the area of ethical decision.

How, then, does one "resolve" the uncertainty? One obtains a nonintellectual resolution through passion, interest, inwardness, and concern. Whether pleasure is the good, or duty is the good, or following Christ is the good, etc., is not intellectually ascertainable. Yet if one passionately gives himself to the task of actualizing one of these alternatives in his *existence*, he may find that X (whichever it may be) is right (or good, etc.) for *him*. But the important point here is that the condition for such certitude (as distinct from rational and objective certainty) is passionate inwardness, not reflection. The problem is, therefore, "resolved" by an existential choice, a leap.[3] Reflection increases the multiplicity and brings objective uncertainty. Passionate choice reduces the multiplicity which always remains at the intellectual level to a unity at the existential level, and brings a subjective certitude, but always in a temporary and insecure way. Thus, reason has its limits, beyond which one must make a passional leap. Whether or not the leap was the "right" one or "true" one, no man could ever *know*.

Kierkegaard's view is also in opposition to all who argue that further reflection, consideration of all the data, etc., will reveal common, *objective values*. As far as I can determine, Kierkegaard neither affirms

[3] *Postscript*, p. 105.

nor denies that values have phenomenally or ontically objective status. His position seems to be that, even if values did possess such status, who could *know* it, except, perhaps, God? And, especially, who could know which actions, characteristics, etc., were valuable, and which were not? Who could know which were right and which were wrong? Intelligence is neutral on such issues. It can make a case for both sides, and for all the positions in between too. And to simply decree that a *moral* intelligence could resolve moral perplexity is begging the issue. Such a maneuver also confuses two realms: thought and reality. These are not, as Hegel said, identical; they are, rather, with one exception to be noted later, absolutely separate.[4] The former deals with idealities which "exist" only for one's thought, as possibilities. The latter concerns existence which cannot be comprehended by objective thought.[5] One cannot, then, by greater reflection, find *one* clear theory which may be shown to be right on matters of existence. All one finds are various alternatives, each of which is rationally plausible.

Thus, we are, precisely because of the empirical data (when fully considered), involved in ethical disagreement. This is so because what one believes concerning ethical matters (and all matters having to do with human existence) is a function of one's passion, interest, and subjectivity. As long as there are varying passions, in unique individuals, there will be varying views. Similarly, ethical agreement (to the extent to which that is possible) is a function of passional likeness among subjects. Ethical judgments, then, are *interested* judgments. They are, Kierkegaard suggested, non-cognitive. This is not to say that they are nonsense, however. For although they are not objectively meaningful, they are subjectively meaningful. They are expressive of a man's passion, interests, and concerns.[6]

I anticipate an objection: "But was not Kierkegaard a Christian? Did he not speak as a religious man? Did he not say that the Christian mode of existence was the highest? Did he not think of the Stages as being progressive steps? And did he not urge his readers to make the progression from the aesthetic, through the ethical, and into the religious?" Yes, Kierkegaard said things of this sort, and spoke from the religious mode when he said them. But this is precisely the point. His utterances of this type were made from the standpoint of a reli-

---

[4] *Ibid.*, pp. 112, 283, 296.
[5] *Ibid.*, p. 274.
[6] *Ibid.*, p. 279.

gious man. Therefore, they were *interested* judgments. This does not contradict the views of Kierkegaard which I expounded earlier. For I insisted throughout that those views (e.g., that no one mode of existence was the right one, etc.) were made from a disinterested, neutral standpoint. Kierkegaard's brilliance (some have held) lies in the fact that he saw that there were at least two types of reflection and their appropriate forms of discourse. There is, first, the reflection (and discourse) of the interested man. This does not require much perspicuity or practice. All men can speak interestedly. There is, second, disinterested, neutral reflection (and its form of discourse). This requires training and a maximization of the intellect. Perhaps few achieve it, and perhaps only on occasions. Yet it is a genuine possibility.

Thus, Kierkegaard's point remains intact. From a disinterested, cognitive standpoint, there is always a multiplicity of alternatives on any issue. From such a standpoint, all possible modes of existence can be given equal rational plausibility. Hence, which is right can never be known.

II

I turn now to the second issue, which flows directly from the first. This, it may be remembered, is the matter of intersubjective validity of ethical judgments. The following discussion is based upon a long chapter of the *Postscript*.[7]

Kierkegaard's discussion may be summed up in the following theses: "The ethical requirement is imposed upon each individual, and when it judges, it judges each individual by himself ... This implies that there is no immediate relationship, ethically, between subject and subject."[8]

Kierkegaard attaches a double meaning to the word 'ethical'. The first meaning is that which is commonly associated with ethics or

---

[7] *Ibid.*, pp. 267–322.

[8] *Ibid.*, pp. 282, 285. I have earlier ("Some Misinterpretations of Kierkegaard," Chapter I) warned against taking the views of the pseudonymous authors to be Kierkegaard's own. Kierkegaard himself stressed this point. Nevertheless, he also held the *Postscript* (and *Fragments*) to have a special status between the purely aesthetic works and the religious writings. He says, for example, that he has affixed his name as editor, which he did not do for any of the strictly pseudonymous works. Hence, we may, I believe, hold that, while the *Fragments* and *Postscript* do not express the reflection and discourse of an interested religious man, they do express that of a disinterested man dealing with a problem.

morals. The second meaning refers to *that which is existent*, rather than merely an object of thought. Perhaps 'behavioral' or 'existential' are better terms in this second sense of 'ethical'. Kierkegaard makes some pertinent remarks about the ethical in the second sense, but these comments also have an important bearing upon the ethical when considered from the standpoint of morality. Let us see what these are. We may use some of Kierkegaard's statements as a kind of outline for this purpose.

1. "From the poetic and intellectual standpoint, possibility is higher than reality, the aesthetic and the intellectual being disinterested."[9]

By 'possibility' Kierkegaard means the realm of the non-existent, or that which "exists" for thought alone. A possibility is an essence, or ideal, or that which may be conceived and reflected upon. By 'reality', on the other hand, Kierkegaard means the realm of the existential, that which actually exists.

Aesthetic and intellectual enterprises, where disinterestedness and objectivity are involved (in the sense that one's existence is not involved), are carried on in the realm of possibility. To have knowledge is to be able to have that which is known "exist" for one's thought. If one merely experienced something without reflecting upon it, this would not be knowledge. Thus, from the intellectual standpoint, possibility is higher than reality, since intelligence cannot manipulate actual objects, existents, and experiences, but can manipulate thoughts about objects, existents, and experiences. Furthermore, in the realm of the intelligible, the greater the degree of disinterestedness and objectivity, the more precise is the knowledge. The thinker who best fulfils his task as a thinker is he who minimizes the influence of his own passions, interests and concerns, with respect to his thinking.

2. "Ethically regarded, reality is higher than possibility."[10]

From the ethical (behavioral and moral) standpoint, that which is real, actual, existent, is of greater significance than that which is merely ideal or possible. E.g., there is nothing moral about being able to talk about morality as a possibility. But to concretely actualize the possibility and *become* a moral man (however 'moral' is defined) is a different matter. Thus, the ethical proposes to do away with the disinterestedness of the realm of possibility by making existence the primary realm and "worthy of infinite interest." The ethical has to

---

[9] *Ibid.*, p. 282.
[10] *Ibid.*, p. 284.

do with the concerns and interests of the subject's existence. Therefore, the ethical is in opposition to all attempts to merely contemplate man in general, or to contemplate the world in this fashion – an act which keeps man or the world in the realm of ideality, rather than in the realm of existence. To contemplate humanity in a system (whether from a metaphysical or a moral standpoint) is, therefore, impossible, since all attempts to contemplate anyone but one's self are endeavors which are carried on in the realm of ideality, and have nothing to do with existence. "There is only one kind of ethical contemplation, namely, self-contemplation."[11] This contemplation, however, is not to be confused with rational cognition.

Hence, it may be affirmed that ethics, whether considered descriptively or normatively, must always center about the individual. It is the individual and not mankind who receives the imperative (a self-imposed imperative) to exist ethically.

Not only is the ethical requirement imposed upon each individual, but when the ethical requirement judges, it judges each individual by himself. This is so because the ethical is internal to each individual. It has as its *locus* the being or selfhood of each individual. Therefore, it cannot be observed or judged by an outsider. The ethical demand can only be actualized by each individual, who alone knows what it is that "moves within him."

Before the ethical life of a person became a reality to him, he was able to know it in a conceived form, as a possibility. When he actualized the possibility, it became a reality for him. But no individual can have knowledge about another person's reality unless, in coming to know it, he conceives it. But as soon as he conceives the reality of another person, he transforms it from a reality in that person's life into a possibility for his own thought. And it is impossible to incorporate *another's existence* into one's own. Thus, no one knows another person's reality or existence. He only knows ideas or thoughts about the other person's reality. The *reality itself* is not known, is never conceivable, by another. Only thoughts about the reality may be known.

With respect to the reality of everyone external to one's self, then, one can "get hold of it" only through conceiving it. In order to get hold of it actually, one would have to make himself into the other person and make his reality one's own. But this is impossible. One

---

[11] *Ibid.*, p. 284.

cannot so acquire the actual existence of another person. In other words, when any reality, say another individual, is external to myself, I can appropriate it only by thinking it. To acquire it actually, I would have to be able to make myself into him and make his reality my own. At the realm of existence such a procedure is impossible. I can appropriate thoughts about another's reality, but not his reality itself.

The upshot of the matter is: There is no immediate ethical relationship between one individual and another.[12] Therefore, any individual can question only himself ethically. None can question another. None can judge another. This is true because, again, no individual can understand another except as a possibility, an ideality, and this understanding may not conform to the actual concrete existence of the other. Another's thoughts may be conceived. His existence may not. For existence itself is not (in any objective sense) conceivable. It just *is*. Hence, each individual is isolated and exists by himself with respect to his ethical requirement. Thus, none can legislate for another concerning his existence and behavior. Therefore, the attempt to find intersubjectively valid ethical judgments ('One ought to do . . .') is futile. There are, and can be, no such judgments.

III

In this section, I would like to show how one might attempt to defend Kierkegaard's views by reformulating the Kierkegaardian position on the two issues, conjointly (with emphasis upon the second), in other terms. For this purpose I shall use, as an outline, two sentences from another context of the *Postscript*.[13]

1. "A logical system is possible."

With respect to thinking, as distinguished from existing or behaving, common norms may be established to which all thinking must conform. Some logicians have conceived the task of logic to be to provide such norms. Logic, in this view, is not a descriptive study of the way in which people *do* think. It is, rather, a prescriptive study of the way in which people *ought to* think.[14]

But, of course, even in the effort to provide norms for thinking, the

---

12 *Ibid.*, p. 285.
13 *Ibid.*, p. 99. My use of these statements does not follow Kierkegaard's exposition of them.
14 I am aware that this view of logic in terms of *thinking*, etc., is not too well-received by many present-day logicians.

content of thought may not be prescribed, but only the method or form. Being logical has nothing to do with the content of one's statements. Thus, the norms provided by logic refer merely to the structure of thinking. If one follows the rules, his thought is logical. If the rules are violated, one's thought becomes illogical. The difference between being logical or illogical, then, has to do with the presence or lack of such characteristics as contradictoriness, etc.

2. "An existential system is impossible."

We may agree, then, that the act of establishing a normative procedure for thinking is an entirely appropriate one. However, some might hold that with respect to methods of *behaving*, no norms may be established to which all behavior must conform. This is so because behavior has to do with the realm of existence, rather than the realm of thought. Behavior refers to that which is existent, not that which is an ideal entity. And, whereas it is appropriate to prescribe rules for correct thinking, it is not appropriate to prescribe rules for correct behavior.

Why is this so? A thought, that which "exists" for reflection, may possess a kind of commonness. That is, I am able to think the thoughts of another, provided that they are clearly expressed and that I have a mental capacity sufficient to understand them. But no similar commonness with respect to the existence of individual selves external to one's own may be found. Hence, whereas I can think the thoughts of another, and can even think thoughts *about* his existence, I cannot think his *existence*. His existence is not amenable to thought. Ideas about his existence are amenable to thought, but one can never know whether the ideas actually "correspond" to his existence. Thus, the existence of another resists being translated from the realm of the existential to the realm of thought or reflection. No matter how hard I might try to think his existence, I cannot succeed, as such a procedure would involve a transformation from the realm of reality or existence to the realm of ideality or reflection, which is impossible. The same applies to impersonal objects. Anything which actually exists, externally to any given subject, cannot be thought, even though one might have probable ideas about the existent object.

Since I cannot think another's existence, I cannot truly know it either. Knowledge has to do with the realm of reflection. I can know ideas or the concepts and thoughts which sentences express. But I cannot strictly know anything which is existent, except my own self.

Consequently, each individual is an isolated self. His existence is peculiar to him, and is not shared with any other existent self, not even those who are most closely associated with him. This is so, again, because no individual can appropriate the existence of another individual to himself. The other always remains a separate self and maintains his own being.

Since each individual is an isolated self, and since no individual can know the existence of another, it follows (some might hold) that no individual may prescribe as to how another individual ought to act. Rules of *behaving* are, thus, inappropriate. Whereas a logical system (prescribed rules for thinking) is possible, a system of ethics (prescribed rules for existing or behaving) is impossible. One can only prescribe rules where there is a common quality shared by all who participate in the endeavor, or, at least, all who can meet the requirements. The realm of thought permits this common quality. The realm of existence does not.

With respect to existing, therefore, each individual must establish his own rules. No one can legislate for another. No one can truly know what is appropriate for any other individual than himself. Since each individual participates only in his own existence, he can only prescribe as to the way in which he (himself) must act. The effort to establish any sort of science of ethics, on the one hand, or a codified morality, on the other, is, therefore, entirely inappropriate. For, since each individual is an isolated self, no one can know what is right or wrong for any other existent self. He can only (according to this view) know this about himself.

I anticipate another question: "How can an individual know what is right or wrong even for himself?" Two questions are implied here: (*a*) If he can know only thoughts, how can he know anything with respect to any existence, even his own? (*b*) How can he know *for certain* which actions (etc.) are right and which are wrong? One might suggest the following answers. (*a*) Any individual is, of course, more than an intellect. He is a synthesis of knowing, imagining, feeling, etc., in existence. Therefore he can, with respect to his own synthesis, have an awareness of matters pertaining to his behavior or existence. This is so because in his own case, and only then, are the subject who knows and the object known identical. (*b*) He cannot know for certain which actions are right and which are wrong, etc. He can only posit certain modes of behaving as being more "right" than others, upon the basis of his relative and limited awareness. No objective certainty is possible here. Furthermore, many factors may enter into his account of what is right.

IV

In this chapter, I do not claim (nor have I done so in previous chapters) that Kierkegaard is right on these matters. In fact, I believe that his ethical theory contains many serious flaws. However, my main concern has been to attempt to state what Kierkegaard in fact held, since here (as in other areas) his views have often been misunderstood.

CHAPTER IV

KIERKEGAARD AND THE MEANINGFULNESS
OF RELIGIOUS STATEMENTS

During the past thirty-five or so years, there has taken place, in philosophical circles, a questioning of the meaningfulness of religious statements. The philosophical position known as logical positivism, or, as some prefer, logical empiricism, achieved notorious fame by its thesis: Religious statements (along with metaphysical, ethical, and aesthetic propositions) are meaningless. Whether or not the discussion has yielded an adequate solution of all problems, it has not been entirely irrelevant. On the contrary, it has extreme relevance for the theologian or the philosopher of religion. And I do not see how a serious attempt at theology, or philosophy of religion, can fail to take cognizance of the philosophical controversy. I say this even though I am fully aware that the movement is not quite as vigorous as it once was and that it has been somewhat superseded by what is loosely referred to as Oxford analysis.

My topic, then, is the status of religious statements. Are they meaningful or not? Or, since there is not merely one kind, which of them are meaningful and which (if any) meaningless? In Section I, I shall schematically classify various types of religious statements, or sentences which purport to be statements, in contrast with sentences which, clearly, are not statements. As we shall see, of those sentences which purport to be statements, some among them are problematical and peculiar. The problem of meaningfulness arises in connection with these. In Section II, I shall state the views of philosophical analysts who have maintained that these problematical sentences are meaningless, and I shall attempt to show why this conclusion was reached. (I shall here ignore the refinements which individual philosophers have made on this doctrine, as they are not important for our purposes.) Before turning to an attempted resolution of the problem I shall, in Section III, present R. G. Collingwood's doctrine of absolute presuppositions. Finally, in Section IV, I shall use Collingwood's doctrine, though not his specific views concerning it, along with some views of Kierkegaard to suggest a possible answer as to the status of religious assertions of the problematical type.

First, some definitions are needed. By 'religious sentences' I mean: (a) sentences which are found within such contemporary religions as Judaism or Christianity; (b) *all kinds* of such sentences, not merely those which refer to the deity or those which are creedal utterances, etc. By 'statement' I mean an indicative sentence which expresses an assertion, which is intended to be literally interpreted, and which may be appropriately labeled either 'true' or 'false'. By 'apparent statement' I mean an indicative sentence which obviously has poetical, etc., rather than literal, intent. By 'non-statement' I mean a sentence or phrase which expresses an ejaculation, exhortation, etc. I add to these, in a tenuous position, a fourth category, 'pseudo-statement', which I shall define later. In my initial discussion pseudo-statements will be included within the class of statements. But, as we shall see, I believe that they must form a separate class, since they lack the characteristics which actual statements possess.

By a 'literal' statement I mean one which is either: (a) a logical truth (and, thus, analytic or tautological) or (b) a factual assertion which is capable of verification in the broad sense. By 'verification in the broad sense' I mean the finding of some actual or possible state of affairs which will confirm or disconfirm the statement. I shall elaborate these points in later parts of the chapter.

So much for preliminaries. I turn now to a rough schematic classification of the various kinds of religious sentences. Whether or not my specific classification is complete is beside the point. For whatever scheme is used, certain sentences will still be peculiar. And here is where the problem of meaningfulness arises.

I

1. There are, of course, many kinds of religious sentences which are *non-statements*. Some of these are: (a) Commands or exhortations: 'Thou shalt not take the name of the Lord thy God in vain' or 'Love one another'. (b) Prayers: 'Lord, have mercy unto me'. (c) Blessings: 'Grace to you and peace from God our Father and the Lord Jesus Christ'. (d) Questions: 'Whence cometh my help?' (e) Ejaculations: 'Woe is me, wretched man that I am!' etc.

Since none of the above utterances (and others like them) are statements, as no assertions are made in them, it would be inappropriate to apply tests for truth or falsity, or to attempt verification of them. We may, therefore, pass by them.

2. Many religious sentences *seem* to be statements but are only *apparent statements*. Some examples are: 'The Lord is my shepherd' or 'Faith moves mountains'. I presume that I do not have to argue the case. I believe that most religious persons would deny that these sentences are to be literally interpreted. Sentences of this type seem to assert something, yet not in the same sense in which 'Jones is my auto mechanic' or 'The Smith Company moves houses' do. In seeking to understand sentences of the above sort, we realize that we must not be too literal, that these are figurative expressions, etc. For example, faith has never been known to move structures such as Mount Everest, but "genuine" faith has been known (it is often said) to perform wonders somewhat similar. Perhaps, indeed, it moves psychical or "spiritual" mountains. And so on, with respect to other apparent statements.

3. I turn now to the class of (actual) *statements*. I distinguish at least five types of religious sentences which *have been held* to be actual statements. As I have already indicated, sentences of the fifth type are problematic.

(1) Many religious statements are *descriptions*. There are, e.g., statements which describe the actions, character, or beliefs of certain religious individuals or groups. Some instances are: 'Many Christians pray', or 'X believes the assertions of the Apostles' Creed', etc. As no particular problems arise in connection with such statements, I move on to the next.

(2) Certain religious statements may be called *explanations*. Some examples are: 'The lack of rain in X is due to the people's sinfulness' (where X is a specified region or country); or 'Britain's military failure of 1916 occurred because farmers planted potatoes on Sunday',[1] etc. Undoubtedly, assertions of this crude kind are seldom made today by sophisticated religious people. However, statements of this *sort* are often encountered. It is possible to test these explanatory hypotheses for validity. Sufficient tests might lead one to believe that there is or is not a connection between, say, the people's sinfulness and rainfall, or between Sunday planting and military failures. To be sure, we may

---

[1] Bertrand Russell, *Unpopular Essays* (New York: Simon & Schuster, 1950), p. 75.

not obtain certainty. This, however, is not the point. As Hume (and others) have emphasized, matter-of-fact statements are never certain.

(3) Some religious statements are *historical statements*. We might (roughly) divide them into two (or more) groups. (a) Some historical statements cause no further problems with respect to verification than those which are found in the case of non-religious historical assertions. Instances of these might be: 'Jesus was born in Bethlehem', 'The apostle Paul was imprisoned', etc. Admittedly, the evidence is scanty. But so is it, in a sense, with respect to judgments about, say, Socrates. And, of course, statements of this kind are also only probable. But, at least, one would know what to look for as evidence by which to assess some "degree" of probability. (b) Other historical statements are more difficult to confirm. Examples are: 'Jesus healed paralytics instantaneously', or 'Jesus arose from the dead', etc. Perhaps, *in practice*, such sentences cannot be verified. But they are certainly not unverifiable *in principle*. Again, one would know what to look for if one had been there at the time of the supposed resurrection, or the healings. (I pass over the spiritual interpretation of the resurrection.)

(4) Certain religious statements might be called *autobiographical statements*, or, perhaps, testimonies. Examples of these are: 'I am persuaded that nothing can separate us from the love of Christ', or 'I am convinced that Christ died for me', etc. Sentences of this kind are somewhat similar to both historical statements and descriptions. But they are more limited than either of those kinds of statements are. They characterize certain attitudes, passions, concerns, and convictions of various individuals. They are not "emotive" utterances, however, since it is possible to confirm the statements. One could find some state of affairs in the world, e.g., the asserter's beliefs or actions, which provides confirmation of the statements.

(5) I turn, finally to the last type of religious sentences which have, traditionally, been held to be statements. Our main problem arises in connection with these. Perhaps some examples will reveal the difficulty: 'God exists', 'God created the world', 'God is triune', 'Jesus is the Son of God' (or 'Jesus is divine'), 'God loves us', 'God has given men free will', 'The Holy Spirit descended upon them', 'There is a life after death of the body', etc.

Sentences such as these purport to be statements. Most religious people who utter such sentences would believe them not to be disguised exhortations, ejaculations, etc. Nor would they be content to say that they are only apparent statements. (Some religious people, of course, would.) And, since they are not descriptive, explanatory, historical, or autobiographical statements, they must form a separate class by themselves. What should they be called? Let us withhold a label for the time being.

More important than a name is the status which such sentences possess. Surely sentences of type (5) are not statements, according to the criteria to which all other statements are subjected. Consider: Actual statements, remember, are those which are confirmable (or disconfirmable) by some state of affairs which warrants the truth (or falsity) of the statements. Sentences of type (5) are not so confirmable – or, even, disconfirmable (as will be shown in Section II). Thus, if they are held to be actual statements, then 'statement' will mean something different, in this case, from what it normally does. Hence one is faced with a decision. Either: (a) the sentences in (5) are not statements; or (b) our usual definition of 'statement' is not correct. The religious man hesitates to assert (a). Yet, if (b) is espoused, then 'statement' will now have two meanings: (i) a normal one which has been given clarity, consistency, and adequacy by the tools of logical and philosophical analysis; and (ii) a peculiar religious meaning which denies the characterizations possessed by the usual one. But if one must resort to this maneuver, then some sentences will be statements by the religious criterion but (at the same time) non-statements by the normal criterion. But, now, what sense does it make to still use the word 'statement' for such sentences? Are we not "trying to have our cake and eat it too"?

II

A view which has gained rather wide acceptance in recent years among philosophical analysts runs as follows:

(A) Sentences of type (5) are not confirmable.
(1) Rational demonstration does not prove them.
(2) Religious experience does not confirm them.
(3) They are unverifiable in principle.
(B) Sentences of type (5) are not falsifiable.
(C) The resort to revelation, faith, etc., fails to provide a third alternative.

Hence: Since only verifiable (or falsifiable) sentences are meaningful, sentences of type (5) are cognitively meaningless.[2]

---

[2] This position is discussed in A. J. Ayer's *Language, Truth, and Logic*. A. Flew and A. Macintyre (eds.), *New Essays in Philosophical Theology* (New York: Macmillan Co., 1955).

The view deserves a fair run for its money. I shall act as its advocate, by giving content to the above structure. The philosophical analyst argues as follows:

(A) Sentences of type (5) are not confirmable. Take the sentence 'God exists'. (That is, he exists actually, and not merely for thought.) Obviously, as far as grammar is concerned, this is a proper statement. However, grammar is not the only criterion by which to judge whether or not a sentence is meaningful. 'Happiness travels at the speed of 60 miles per hour', is grammatically proper. Yet it has no clear meaning. In a similar way, it is appropriate to ask whether 'God exists' has any meaning. And, of course, if it is the case that 'God exists' is meaningless, then 'God does not exist' is equally meaningless – as Ayer has shown.[3] One cannot, therefore, escape the problem by professing atheism, for, if the affirmation of a sentence is absurd, then the denial is equally absurd.

(1) Rational demonstration does not prove sentences of type (5) to be true. Sufficient labors have been spent upon the traditional arguments for the existence of God to show that they are not valid. Even theologians and philosophers of religion have admitted this.[4] A few fallacies in reasoning might be mentioned. The sentence 'God exists' is held, in the ontological argument and in variants of the cosmological argument, to be logically necessary; but no existential proposition can be logically necessary. And the argument from analogy, which occurs in the teleological argument, is shaky, since arguments from analogy never bridge the leap from the finite evidence to the infinite existent.

One might object that although these particular arguments, and all variants of them, are invalid, the conclusion may, nevertheless, be true. Very well, what other means shall we attempt in order to discover whether or not 'God exists' is true?

(2) Let us try the religious experience claim. Some religious people profess to have knowledge of the existence of God upon the basis of direct experience of God. They say that our knowledge of God rests upon the revelation of his personal presence, or that our knowledge of God comes through a direct, personal encounter or confrontation with him. It must be noticed that people who talk this way do not simply assert that they had an unusual experience. They claim to have an experience of *God*.

---

[3] Ayer, *op. cit.*, chap. vi.
[4] I shall not rehash old arguments. If the reader is unconvinced, I refer him to H. J. Paton, *The Modern Predicament* (New York: Macmillan Co., 1955), chaps. xii–xiv.

But this procedure is incapable of establishing what it hopes to establish. Just as the assertion that God exists cannot be shown to be warrantable by means of rational demonstration, so it cannot be shown to be warrantable by the religious experience claim. For all that the sentence 'I have had an experience of God' can certify is that I have had certain feelings, sensations, etc. It cannot confirm the further assertion that God exists. The method of religious experience can, thus, give one a feeling or "inner assurance" that God exists or may exist, but it cannot confirm that God does, in fact, exist. In order for the assertion 'God exists' to be warrantable, it would have to be inter-subjectively testable. Yet the possibility of such testability is precisely what proponents of the religious experience claim deny. They maintain that the way of knowing God through religious experience is unique. They say that one cannot know what the experience of God is until one has had it. And apparently only a few are privileged to have it.

Thus, the religious experience method never answers the question: 'How can you know when anyone has had an experience of God?' There are certain tests by which I can know, with a high degree of probability, as to whether or not I have had, say an experience of flying in a jet airplane. But what tests can be devised by which I can know whether or not I have had an experience of God? The proponents of the religious-experience claim are silent here. In place of tests they posit the notion of an "immediacy" of knowledge which is supposed to carry its own guaranty of confirmation. But, surely, many people who claim to have had genuine experiences of something or other have been wrong! Therefore, the religious-experience method cannot confirm the assertion, 'I have had direct experiences of God, and God exists'. The most which it can confirm is the assertion, 'I have had some kind of peculiar experience by which it seems to me that God exists', and this is something very different from the first sentence.

Other methods which have been used in the attempt to confirm the sentence 'God exists' (the moral argument, etc.) bring us no nearer to a satisfactory conclusion. My purpose here is not to give an exhaustive treatment of the alternatives with respect to the single sentence 'God exists' but to indicate the kinds of problems which one encounters with sentences of type (5). It may be objected that I have unfairly selected the most difficult sentence of this group. However, the other sentences of this type presuppose the sentence 'God exists' and would be meaningless if this one were no statement at all. In fact, many of the others include the assertion of God's existence when attributing qualities or action to God. Thus, in actual practice, religious people think of the sentence 'God loves us' as expressing both 'God exists' and 'He loves us'. Hence the problems reappear.

(3) The primary difficulty with sentences of type (5) arises not merely because such assertions are unverifiable *in practice;* rather, it lies in the fact that such sentences are not even verifiable *in principle.* There is no conceivable way by which one could test such sentences. If a sentence refers to God, e.g., we not only face the problem that we cannot find some actual state of affairs by which to confirm it. We are further handicapped by the fact that we could not conceive of any possible method of verification. 'There are insects on Mars' is perhaps, at present, unverifiable in practice. Yet, if we could some day reach the planet and survive, we would, at least, know what to look for in order to confirm the sentence. It is, thus, verifiable in principle, though not in practice. The theological sentences which we have been considering are not only unverifiable in practice but also in principle. One cannot imagine any conceivable state of affairs by which to confirm such sentences.

(B) Thus far, we have primarily dealt with the question: What state of affairs would one have to find in order to *confirm* such sentences as 'God exists', etc.? We found that such sentences are incapable of verification (or confirmation). Let us, now, ask the question with respect to *falsification.* That is: What state of affairs would one have to find which would constitute a falsification of such sentences as 'God exists'? In other words, what events would have to occur in order to be a sufficient reason for stating 'There is no God' or 'God does not love us', etc.?

Antony Flew has discussed this problem with respect to the sentence, 'God loves us as a father loves his children'.[5] Many religious people hold this sentence to be true. But suppose that we see a child dying of cancer. His earthly father is greatly concerned and expresses his love for the child by attempting every possible method of providing help for him. But God, the "heavenly Father," shows no apparent sign of concern. At this point, religious people often qualify the assertion by adding, "Well, God's love is not merely human love," or "God's ways, including his way of loving, are inscrutable." Thus, the severe sufferings of the child are held to be compatible with the assertion that 'God loves us as a father loves his children' – plus the qualifications. But

---

[5] Flew and Macintyre, *op. cit.,* pp. 98–99.

if the sentence must be qualified – 'God's love is different; he has reasons we know not of', etc. – why maintain it? What is this affirmation of God's love worth if it must be so qualified as to mean something different from the original sentence? What would have to happen in order to persuade and entitle us to say 'God does *not* love us'? What state of affairs would have to occur in order to constitute a falsification of the assertion that God loves us? Religious people maintain that no conceivable experience could falsify sentences of this sort.

Thus we are left with the peculiar situation whereby *all* states of affairs are held to be commensurate with an assertion such as 'God loves us as a father loves his children', and similar assertions. To a neutral observer, certain states of affairs would seem to show that God loves us, while others would indicate that he does not love us. To the religious person, however, there is no conceivable state of affairs which would be a demonstration that God does not love us. Even innocent children, dying in agony, are held to be no falsification of the sentence 'God loves us'. But if *every* state of affairs is compatible with the sentence 'God loves us', then no falsification is possible. And if no falsification is possible, then the sentence seems to have no straightforward meaning, and is, hence, cognitively meaningless.

Thus, whether we attempt to verify or falsify a sentence of type (5), we note that there are no criteria which are acceptable. It would seem, therefore, that such sentences are cognitively meaningless. One need not thereby deny that such assertions may possess some other status. They may, for example, be expressive of certain emotions, feelings, and attitudes which are felt by the one who utters them, and which, perhaps, evoke similar emotions and attitudes in others.

(C) There have been various attempts to completely escape the predicament in which we find ourselves. These, too, have failed. Some, e.g., have said that sentences of type (5) are known to be true by revelation. They are "revealed truths," rather than natural truths, and, therefore, not subject to verification. But this is a fruitless effort. For sophisticated religious people deny that any propositions are presented in revelation, and naive religious people must posit the notion of inspiration by which to give the revealed propositions the status of truth, forgetting that the notion of inspiration itself is impossible of verification.

Other religious people suggest still another alternative. They maintain that there are "truths of faith" as over against "truths of reason." In this view it is appropriate to seek verification of sentences which fall into the "reason category, but it is inappropriate to seek verification of those which are in the "faith" group. The meaning of faith, they tell us, is to believe where no proof is possible. Yet beliefs are often notoriously incredible, as well as incompatible at times. Apparently some religious people once believed that Joshua command- ed the moon to stand still, or that the bodies of the saints were raised after Jesus' death and appeared to many people. Where is one to draw the line as to what may or may not be believed? How can one know that the belief that God created the world is any more true than the belief that Jesus spoke to demons and was answered? Furthermore, various religions seem to hold incompatible views with respect to the nature or activity of the deity. What certifies the Christian view, or particular opinions within the Christian view? (And the same question may be asked with regard to any other religion.)

In conclusion, it may be affirmed that religious statements of the first four types are meaningful. But religious sentences of type (5) are meaningless.

Thus runs the argument against permitting the status of statements to religious sentences of the fifth type. Can we "save" such sentences from the onslaught? Before answering the question, I would like to turn, briefly, to some interesting insights of R. G. Collingwood, which might be used to suggest a possible path toward an "answer." In Section III, I shall merely state Collingwood's views. In Section IV, I shall apply one of these doctrines toward a possible "solution" of our problem by way of some views held by Kierkegaard.

III

The particular views of Collingwood which are of relevance for the issue at hand are found in *An Essay on Metaphysics*.[6] The opening pages of the work are devoted to a consideration of Aristotle's meta- physics, in which Collingwood finds three definitions of metaphysics: (i) Metaphysics is the science of pure being. (ii) Metaphysics is the science of the highest being. (iii) Metaphysics is the science which deals with the presuppositions underlying ordinary science. Colling- wood argues that the first of these definitions cannot be true, as a

---

[6] R. G. Collingwood, *An Essay on Metaphysics* (London: Oxford University Press, 1940).

science of pure being is a contradiction in terms. He dismisses the second definition. He affirms the third as being the proper one, and his book is an effort to explain its meaning.[7] As distinct from metaphysics, the science of pure being – or attempts at it – may be called ontology. It does not designate any actual science. It merely refers to the mistakes which people have made. Thus, by rejecting ontology, Collingwood develops a doctrine of "metaphysics without ontology."[8]

Metaphysics, then, for Collingwood, is the science which deals with the presuppositions underlying ordinary science, that is, any science other than metaphysics (and in the broad sense of science, i.e., any organized body of knowledge). However, certain presuppositions are of greater interest to the metaphysician than others. These are *absolute*, as distinct from *relative*, presuppositions.

A relative presupposition is one which may stand relatively to one question as its presupposition and relatively to another question as its answer. Collingwood's homely example is that of a man measuring the distance between two points with an old tape. In asking the question, 'What is the distance between these two points?' he is making a presupposition, namely, 'My tape is accurate (to a certain degree)'. This presupposition is also an answer to another question: 'Is my tape accurate?' The answer that the tape is accurate was obtained by checking it with some more reliable measure. Thus relative presuppositions may be verified. Since they are answers to questions, they are also propositions, or statements, as well as presuppositions. Therefore, with respect to them it is appropriate to ask: 'Are they true (or false)?'[9]

An absolute presupposition, however, is "one which stands, relatively to all questions to which it is related, as a presupposition, never as an answer."[10] Collingwood's illustration (again a commonsensical one) is as follows. Suppose that one were to talk to a pathologist about a certain disease and were to ask him what is the cause of the event, *E*, which occurs in this disease. He would answer that the cause of *E* is *C*, and he would perhaps recommend some authority on the matter. One finds in the course of the discussion that the pathologist, as well as his authority, assumed that *E* has a cause before it was known what the cause is. If you then asked him: "Why did you assume that it has

---

[7] *Ibid.*, pp. 11–16.
[8] *Ibid.*, p. 17.
[9] *Ibid.*, pp. 29–30.
[10] *Ibid.*, p. 31.

a cause?" you would probably be told: "Because everything that happens has a cause." If you then asked how, in turn, *this* is known, you would here encounter one of the pathologist's absolute presuppositions, and you would be told that this is not something which we can prove or verify. We simply have to take it for granted. Thus absolute presuppositions are unverifiable, that is to say, *they are not propositions or statements*. The distinction between truth and falsity, or verifiability and unverifiability, does not apply to them at all.[11]

Metaphysics, then, for Collingwood, is the attempt to find out what *absolute presuppositions* have been held by certain persons or groups of persons on certain occasions and in the course of certain "pieces" of thinking. To ask whether or not absolute presuppositions are true, or upon what evidence they may be accepted, is to engage in pseudo-metaphysics.[12] Metaphysical questions and presuppositions are, thus, historical questions and presuppositions. The metaphysician merely attempts to state what presuppositions were made by various scientists in various periods of history. And he may attempt to compare presuppositions and inquire as to how certain ones grew out of others as the result of internal strain.[13]

In a section entitled "Examples," Collingwood discusses the absolute presupposition 'God exists' as an instance (among others) of the kind of presuppositions which have been held in history. He considers the question with reference to the Christian patristic writers, to whom, Collingwood believes, the existence of God was an absolute presupposition of all thinking done by reflective Christians, especially that which was done in natural science.[14] Since their affirmation, 'God exists', is an absolute presupposition, it follows that it is not a proposition or statement. It is, therefore, neither true nor false. And it can neither be proved nor disproved. It can only be presupposed or believed in.[15]

Collingwood then traces the history of this absolute presupposition back to the pre-Christian Greek era and shows how it, along with certain subordinate presuppositions, was held, knowingly or unknowingly, by natural scientists throughout the course of their work.[16] This is an interesting discussion. However, I shall not summarize it because it is, for various reasons, somewhat beside the point for the

[11] *Ibid.*, pp. 31–32.
[12] *Ibid.*, p. 47.
[13] *Ibid.*, pp. 7off.
[14] *Ibid.*, p. 186.
[15] *Ibid.*, p. 188.
[16] *Ibid.*, pp. 213–27.

topic at hand, which is not the relationship of the presupposition of the existence of God to natural science but the significance of this presupposition, and others like it, for theology or philosophy of religion.

So much, then, for Collingwood. I turn, next, to an application of the doctrine of absolute presuppositions to our problem concerning the status of religious sentences of type (5). In so doing, I must make it clear that I am departing from Collingwood's views. This application of the doctrine was apparently never noted by Collingwood. At least he never discussed the matter. Perhaps this is a result of his belief that absolute presuppositions are peculiar to certain historical eras. Thus, he seems to have thought that 'God exists' was an absolute presupposition for the few centuries before and after Christ, but not for the present day. My application will also depart from this feature of Collingwood's theory.

IV

At the end of Section II, we were left with the view of the philosophical analyst, according to which sentences of type (5) are meaningless and, hence, not genuine statements. Nor are they apparent statements or non-statements. Rather, they are, in his opinion, nonsense. Our task was to see whether religious sentences of type (5) could be "saved" from this fate.

A solution which one might suggest runs as follows;

The philosophical analyst is right in one respect. Sentences of type (5) are not statements. Let us, therefore, remove them from their position as a type under group 3 (statements) and give them a separate classification, group 4, which I have called pseudo-statements. The theologian must "yield" at this point. Why? Because the arguments of the analyst (presented in Section II) are sound. It was there shown that sentences of type (5) cannot be statements by all the ordinary criteria for statements. Why, then, continue the pretense that they, nevertheless, somehow are statements? Intellectual honesty ought to be the rule in theology as well as in other disciplines.

However, according to the proponent of this "solution," the analyst is wrong in another respect. Pseudo-statements are not meaningless. They merely have different criteria for meaningfulness from those of statements. It is true that sentences such as 'God exists', 'God loves us', etc., are not statements (or propositions). It is, therefore, inappropriate to ask whether they are true or false. It is also inappropriate to seek verification, or falsification, of them. This does not destroy their meaningfulness. Such sentences *are* meaningful. But they are meaningful (to use Collingwood's term) as *absolute presuppositions*, and not as statements.

In other words, the existence of God, God's love for man, God's activity in Christ, etc., might be construed as presuppositions (and absolute ones) of all the thinking that is done by Christians not only in natural science but in ethics, theology, and other areas of thought. They are also presuppositions (if one may extend the term) of a certain mode of existence, one which can be characterized and structured by thought. This mode of existence, or way of life, has been called "salvation" or "the new birth."

Now, if we agree with Collingwood that the task of the metaphysician is to discover what absolute presuppositions are, or have been, held and to state them, what is the theologian's task – to explain them, to prove them to be true, to give reasons for them? Obviously not, if it is held that such assertions are absolute presuppositions and not statements. The theologian must, therefore, not yield to the temptation to become apologetic for the absolute presuppositions. He will accept them as sentences which are not to be proved but merely to be supposed or believed in.

Perhaps an illustration is in order. Take the sentence, 'Jesus is God and man' (or 'Jesus is the Son of God', 'Jesus is divine', etc.). Even theologians who have denied that this sentence (or some variant) could be "proved" (whatever that would be) have, nevertheless, thought that one could give rational grounds for the belief that Jesus is divine. They did this by the categories of ontology and with the notion of the second person of the Trinity, e.g. Thus the language of *Logos*, *homoousios*, etc. The categories were not only ontological but supernatural. Thus the two natures doctrine of the creedal formulation.

One might argue that this attempt served a purpose. But to continue it in our day is, in my opinion, utterly fruitless. Hence the theologian (or philosopher of religion) who wishes to preserve the meaningfulness of the sentence 'Jesus is God' (or some variant) must take another approach. One of the alternatives is: to consider such sentences as being absolute presuppositions, not statements. But if this path is followed, then the theologian will not ask: Is it *true* that Jesus is God? How may we find some rational grounds for asserting that sentence to be true? etc. Rather, he will ask: What results from our presupposing that Jesus is God? And have we any means of affirming him as such without the use of supernatural or ontological categories?

The defender of this "solution" holds that it is conceivable that an affirmative answer can be given to the latter question. The task may be achieved if the theologian is content to describe and discuss that which is within experience, rather than beyond it; that which is "natural" rather than "supernatural"; that which is commonsensical rather than ontological; that which may be formulated in statements rather than uttered in perplexing pseudo-statements. He will refrain from asserting problematic sentences of type (5), which, nevertheless, continue to be *held* by him as absolute presuppositions. But his own assertions are not presuppositions. They are, rather, statements. And statements deal with very ordinary and commonsensical matters, such as the mode of existence in which one lives and the concerns and interests of men. Hence no ontological categories are found in the theologian's language. And he will not expound *doctrines* of the Trinity, Incarnation, etc.

This might be put in another way. The theologian will describe the order of possibility and the order of historical being but not the order of ontological objects. Kierkegaard may be of help at this point.[17] A *possible* (or possibility), according to Kierkegaard, is that about which one can have meaningful discourse. Such discourse will be in the form of statements which describe or explicate the possible. A possible, hence, is anything which can be reflected about, anything concerning which one can utter significant propositions. Some possibles elicit interest, concern, and passion. These may be called ethical or behavioral possibles. Now behavioral possibles are never exclusive for one's *thought*. They form a plurality. And one can think and elucidate many possible modes of existence, and with equal rational plausibility. In thought, one can never reduce the multiplicity to a unity. One can never find only one to be true or right and the others false or wrong. Rather, the greater one's intelligence is, the more possibles one can find, or the more plausibility can be given to those which one has already conceived. However, when one seeks to actualize a possible

---

[17] S. Kierkegaard, *Concluding Unscientific Postscript*, trans. D. F. Swenson and W. Lowrie (Princeton, N.J.: Princeton University Press, 1944), pp. 267ff. See also Paul L. Holmer, "Philosophical Criticism and Christology," *Journal of Religion*, XXXIV (1954). 88–100. Professor Holmer arrives at conclusions similar to those presented here. However, he leaves the status of sentences such as 'Jesus is divine', etc., in a somewhat vague position. I *suggest* that they might be held to be absolute presuppositions.

in one's *existence*, he finds that they are exclusive. One can maximally actualize only one at a time.[18]

How does this apply to such sentences as 'Jesus is God' and to the task of the theologian? Christ can be (and was, by Kierkegaard) construed as a kind of possibility. He can be conceived as one who presents a challenge (an existential challenge, if you please) to all men. Because of his life, death, teaching, etc., he commands attention. And having heard of him, many men are influenced to re-examine their lives and some to shift their interests, concerns, and enthusiasms from themselves to him. Christ, himself, actualized a certain mode of existence. The mode which he realized is present to all men as a possibility. For those who choose to actualize it, Christ "becomes" God. I use quotes intentionally. What I mean is: those who actualize the possibility believe him to be God, i.e., believe him to be that which can fully control and captivate one's interests. For those who actualize the possibility, the divinity of Christ is their absolute presupposition. Is he God independently of their supposing him to be so? Who knows? Not only can one not answer the question, but the asking of it is inappropriate. All one can say is that one's supposing him to be God makes him God for one's self. Whether or not he *is* God ("from all eternity") one cannot know, and does not ask.

Hence the discourse of the theologian will include historical statements. These will be, for example, about a man, Jesus, who lived, taught, etc., nearly 2,000 years ago. These are neutral statements which can be believed by religious and non-religious men alike. And, of course, they are only probable, as are *all* historical statements. As I already mentioned, the theologian's discourse will not include ontological assertions, such as sentences of type (5). These are merely supposed or believed in. The theologian's discourse will also include testimonies. He will discuss the transformation of personality which resulted when he and/or others exchanged one passionate interest (in his own existence) for another (an interest in Christ's existence). He will elucidate how such transfer of interests has made men into "new creatures," how it resynthesized the factors of men's personalities. And the theologian's discourse may include exhortations. He will, perhaps, invite others to accept the mode of existence which Christ presented, not because of a "proof" that Christ is God, but simply because others have found Christ capable of maintaining their maxi-

---

[18] This paragraph expresses the "heart" of Kierkegaard's doctrine of the Stages.

mum enthusiasm and passion and because such interest has brought about a new synthesis of personality, a revitalized mode of existence.

The theologian, then, has a more limited task than he has heretofore had. It is to delineate Christ as a possible – a conceivable mode of existence, one alternative among others. The task of the religious man is to transform the possible from a possibility to an actuality in his own existence. With respect to both the theologian and the "ordinary" man, the question 'Is Jesus *really* divine?' etc., does not arise. For both of them, it is an absolute presupposition which stands at the basis of their thinking and their mode of existence. It is significant both for thought and for life.

I have briefly portrayed what might be considered as an alternative way of dealing with religious sentences of type (5) – sentences which I referred to as 'pseudo-statements' and which I transferred from group 3 (statements) to group 4. To those who insist upon the verification of such sentences as a requirement for their meaningfulness, such sentences will remain pseudo-statements, and no more. But to those who adopt the approach which I have suggested, and which comes largely from some insights of Collingwood, with a few hints from Kierkegaard, these sentences might be considered to be absolute presuppositions.

I repeat: In describing the form in which such a view might be developed, I do not imply that I agree with the position. I merely suggest it as a possible alternative. Elsewhere I have given reasons for rejecting it.[19]

---

[19] E. D. Klemke, *Reflections and Perspectives: Essays in Philosophy* (The Hague: Mouton Publishers, 1974), chap. 8.

CHAPTER V

WAS KIERKEGAARD A THEIST?

I

To some readers, the answer to the question which I have posed in the title will seem obvious: "If you mean by a Theist one who believes in the existence of a transcendent God, etc., then of course Kierkegaard was a Theist." And evidence for such an answer can readily be produced by citing Kierkegaard's later religious – or more specifically, Christian – writings which constitute a large part of his works. However, in posing the question, I am referring to certain views expressed primarily in two of Kierkegaard's earlier, more "philosophical" works, the *Philosophical Fragments* and the *Concluding Unscientific Postscript*. And of course, if it could be shown that Kierkegaard did *not* hold a traditional Theistic view in those works, then one might argue that the later religious writings ought to be interpreted in a non-traditional way, one which accords with the conception put forth in the two earlier books. However, this would not be a satisfactory reply to anyone who answered the title-question in the manner I indicated above. For such readers could rightly point out that the *Fragments* and *Postscript* are both among Kierkegaard's pseudonymous works; and they might stress that, in view of Kierkegaard's own comments, the position held in those works should be attributed to the pseudonymous author, Johannes Climacus, and not to Kierkegaard himself. The first of these assertions is undeniably true, and the second has considerable force. Hence, at least for the present, I shall change my original question for another: Was Johannes Climacus a Theist?

   I anticipate at least two responses to this reformulation of the question. To some, the answer to this second question will seem as obvious as the answer to the first: "Yes, of course, Johannes Climacus

was a Theist" – i.e., the views attributed to this pseudonymous author
express a traditional Theistic concept of God. To others, the reformulated question may seem of much less interest than the first, especially
if we are prevented from attributing the views held in the *Fragments*
and *Postscript* to Kierkegaard himself. To these responses I must
reply: First, I hope to show that the supposedly obvious answer to the
second, reformulated question is not obvious at all, and further, that
crucial passages in those works provide good reasons for maintaining
that Climacus was *not* a Theist. Second, I would maintain that, even
if we are ultimately prohibited from attributing Climacus' position to
Kierkegaard, nevertheless, the reformulated question is still one which
is not only interesting but valuable, since it provides a different interpretation of some of the central Christian claims and suggests a novel
view of such matters as the nature of religious language.

With these preliminary comments, I shall proceed as follows. First,
I shall briefly state some of the main theses of the *Fragments*. Second,
I shall examine some of the crucial terms, specifically those of the third
chapter, and distinguish various uses of them. Third, I shall formulate
an hypothesis which is suggested by passages from that work. Fourth,
I shall attempt to show that this hypothesis is supported by the
Postscript as well. The result of the whole will, I believe, establish the
plausibility of my claim that Climacus was not a Theist. (At the end,
I shall briefly return to the matter of Kierkegaard's own view.)

II

On the title-page of his *Philosophical Fragments*[1] Kierkegaard's author
asks three questions: "Is an historical point of departure possible for an
eternal consciousness; how can such a point of departure have any other
than a merely historical interest; is it possible to base an eternal happiness upon historical knowledge?" Since Kierkegaard's author answers
the first question affirmatively and claims to have provided an answer
to the second and third, one might hold that *my* reformulated question
has thereby an affirmative answer. Presumably one would hold such an
opinion because of Kierkegaard's use of expressions such as 'eternal',
etc. However, such a judgment would be rash, for the point at issue is
what meanings Kierkegaard (or his author) gives to these expressions.

[1] Translated by David F. Swenson and revise d by Howard V. Hong (Princeton: Princeton
University Press, 1962). Page numbers in parent heses in this section, refer to this volume.

Hence, let us proceed to a closer examination of the main themes of the book which are relevant to providing an answer to my reformulated question.

Before turning to the text, a few comments are in order. First, the *Fragments* and *Postscript* are, among Kierkegaard's pseudonymous works, those in which he lists himself as responsible for their publication. Second, with regard to the *Fragments*, Kierkegaard held that it could be considered either as an attack or as a defense of Christianity. His aim was to present Christianity as a view of life in a neutral and detached manner. Hence, to read it does not presuppose being a "believer." One can read it and accept *or* reject Christianity. To understand and accept is not the only appropriate response; to understand and reject is fitting too. Third, Kierkegaard's major problem (or that of his author) is set by a commonly held view in Kierkegaard's time and at others, namely, that religious truth is propositional. The *Fragments* present a criticism of this view. The author does not deny that propositions may be involved in articulating Christianity, but faith does not consist in giving assent to them.

I turn now to the text itself. Since I am assuming familiarity with the work by the reader, I shall be brief in my exposition. Kierkegaard's author begins the first chapter with the question: "How far does the Truth admit of being learned?" (p. 11). He contrasts two figures, an idealized Socrates and someone referred to as the Teacher, and two approaches towards answering the question, the "Socratic-Platonic" view and that of Christianity (the latter presented as if it were an invented hypothesis or "project of thought").

In the Socratic view, in order to learn the Truth, one must already know it before it is given to him, for how else could he recognize it as being the Truth? But this seems odd, for then the only ones who can learn the Truth are those who already know it. In order to avoid this paradox, Plato proposed the doctrine of recollection according to which all learning is a form of remembering what one once knew but forgot. In this view, the Truth is grasped by individual insight. The teacher is accidental or incidental; he merely provides the occasion by which the learner can grasp the Truth. The teacher does not give the Truth to the learner but merely elicits it from him. Hence the teacher is only of passing, historical interest, for it is one's own recognition of the Truth that matters. Further, there is no decisive moment in time at which the learner is rescued from ignorance.

In the contrasting view, the Moment in time at which the Truth is revealed is decisive, for the learner is destitute of the Truth up to that very moment at which he learned it. The learner is initially in a state of Error and hence does not merely recall the Truth. Thus the Teacher is essential, in this view, for he not only enables the learner to discover that he is in Error; he also gives the learner the necessary condition for understanding the Truth and by means of this, the Truth as well. The initial state of Error is Sin, not merely ignorance. And the Teacher saves the learner from his captivity and hence is called Redeemer. Because of this the Teacher must never be forgotten by the learner lest he slip back into Error. The Teacher does not merely provide an occasion but is decisive for the atonement which he constitutes. Hence, the learner is a disciple of the Teacher, and in virtue of his relation to the Teacher becomes, through a process of Conversion, a new creature.

In the second chapter of the Fragments, Kierkegaard's author develops the "hypothesis" further and asks us to assume that the Teacher is God (or the God) and the disciple is man. In the Socratic view, the teacher is the accidental occasion for the learner's understanding of himself, and reciprocally the learner is the accidental occasion for the teacher's understanding of himself. But God does not need the learner in order to understand himself. What then motivated him to rescue the learner? God's love is the answer. But a pedogogical problem arises here. Since there is a great difference between God and man, how can God make himself understood and thereby reach the learner? Of the alternatives available, the answer given is: God became a human being, but disguised himself in the form of a suffering servant, rather than appearing in a manner in which he could be directly recognized as God. Thus we have the Miracle.

Kierkegaard's author continues the discussion of his "project of thought" in the third chapter which is perhaps the most crucial one of the book. He again refers to Socrates who, although having been a life-long student of human nature, yet said that he really could not understand himself – which seems to be a paradox. We are told that a paradox is "the source of a thinker's passion," that, since "the highest pitch of every passion is always to will its own downfall," "so it is the supreme passion of the Reason to seek a collision, though this collision must ... prove its undoing," that "the supreme paradox of all thought is to discover something that thought cannot think," and that "this passion is "present in all thinking" (p. 46). And what is it that the Reason collides with? The Unknown, which, since it is not any known thing may be called *"the God"* – "nothing more than a name we assign to it" (p. 49). We cannot demonstrate its existence. The Unknown is "the limit to which the Reason repeatedly comes" and hence is "the absolutely different" (p. 55). But since it is absolutely different, there is no way by which it can be disclosed, for "the Reason cannot even conceive an absolute unlikeness" (p. 55). Thus if a man were to achieve knowledge about the Unknown (the God), he would have to know that it is absolutely unlike him. Since the Reason cannot obtain this knowledge by itself, it would have to obtain it from the God. But even if it were to obtain it, it could not understand it and thus would not actually possess any such knowledge. "For how should the Reason be able to understand what is absolutely different from itself?" (p. 57).

Thus we have here a paradox. "Merely to obtain the knowledge that the God is unlike him, man needs the help of the God; and now he learns that the God is absolutely different from himself. But if the God and man are absolutely different, this cannot be accounted for on the basis of what man derives from the God, for in so far they are akin. Their unlikeness must therefore be explained by what man derives from himself, or by what he has brought upon his own head. But what can this unlikeness be? Aye, what can it be but sin ..." (p. 58). But the consciousness of sin is something which only the God could teach to a man, if the God became a Teacher – which is what the hypothesis maintained. "In order to be man's Teacher, the God proposed to make himself like the individual man, so that he might understand him fully. Thus our paradox is rendered still more appalling, or the same paradox has the double aspect which proclaims it as the Absolute Paradox; negatively revealing the absolute unlikeness of sin, positively by proposing to do away with the absolute unlikeness in absolute likeness" (pp. 58–59).

In the Appendix to Chapter III, Kierkegaard's author maintains that there are two significant responses to the awareness of the paradox: offense and a "happy passion," later identified as Faith. And in the last chapters, he emphasizes that, since Faith is a passion and not a higher level of knowledge, and since the object of Faith is the Teacher himself and not a doctrine, the immediate contemporary disciple has no advantage over the disciple "at second hand" (that is, the disciple of later generations). I shall return to some of the more relevant features of these chapters later.

III

Earlier I stated that the third chapter of the *Fragments* was perhaps the most crucial one. It is also the one which has the greatest bearing upon the thesis which I want to propose. In addition, it is one of the most difficult chapters of the book. Hence before formulating my thesis and presenting grounds for it, I shall turn to an examination of two of the most essential concepts of the chapter, or if you will, the two key terms: 'reason' and 'paradox'. The entire chapter, and indeed the whole book, presupposes an understanding of the various uses of these terms and those uses which are employed by Kierkegaard's author. Since I wish, in both cases, to distinguish several senses, I have deliberately written (above) 'reason', rather than 'the Reason'; similarly for 'paradox'.[2]

I shall begin with 'reason'. I wish to distinguish four senses (or uses) of this term. For convenience, I shall label these the Metaphysical, Epistemological, Logical, and Commonsensical uses (or senses) of the term. I do not claim that there is always a rigid distinction among these senses. Here, as in the case of most classifications, there often occurs in certain contexts an overlap in usage.

(1) The Metaphysical sense. This sense of the term 'reason' is that which we find employed by or attributed to such philosophers as Hegel. It is a technical sense in which reason is conceived as a fundamental constituent or aspect of reality or indeed as reality itself. Its most notable use is found in the Hegelian slogan, "The real is the rational, and the rational is the real." Kierkegaard sometimes uses the term in this sense, but when he does so the occurrence is ironical, with reference to Hegel. The term is not used in this sense when Kierkegaard (or Climacus) presents his own views.

(2) The Epistemological sense. By this sense of the term 'reason', I refer to another technical sense (which may or may not overlap with the first), whereby 'reason' is used in an abstract, "intellectual" sense to designate a special faculty of cognition (as opposed to sensation and the like) which, it is held, provides knowledge which is a priori (as opposed to "mere" empirical knowledge). This sense of the term is

---

[2] In much of what I shall say regarding these uses, I am indebted to lectures by and conversations with Paul L. Holmer. However, since these took place many years ago, I do not claim that my distinctions are the same as his. Furthermore, even if there are parallels, I do not know if he any longer maintains the views which he held at that time. Some of these distinctions were made earlier by David F. Swenson.

that of those philosophers who advocate "the eye of reason," etc. Again, Kierkegaard seldom makes use of this sense of the term, unless it is in reference to other philosophers. And again, the term is not used in this sense by him (or Climacus) when presenting his views.

(3) The Logical sense. This use of 'reason' (often called the "formal" sense) refers to the ability to use – or the practice of using – neutral categories, the rules of discourse, the rules of logical inference, etc., with regard to any conceivable content. In this sense, the term does not imply any specific source of knowledge, nor does it imply any particular values, other than norms of consistency, etc. Just as an honest man and a thief can both employ the rules of arithmetic, so both can employ the laws of logic, however devious the ends may be by their doing so. Furthermore, the use of reason, in this sense, pertains to any subject matter, from the lowly concerns of everyday discourse to the most esoteric realms of scientific treatises. In this sense of 'reason', Kierkegaard – in spite of claims to the contrary – uses reason (not just the word, but its referent) throughout his writings. Indeed, both the *Fragments* and the *Postscript* (among other works) exemplify his being an expert practitioner of reason as an instrument of logicality. Does his (or Climacus') use of the expression 'the Reason' in the *Fragments* designate this sense? In part, I believe it does, as we shall see when I turn to the various uses of the term 'paradox'.

(4) The Commonsensical sense. By this sense of the term 'reason', I am referring to the very ordinary, concrete, and practical sense in which the term is used to designate – as the label implies – just "plain" common sense, including not only certain beliefs but also various commonly recognized values which, some would maintain, are held or should be held by all "reasonable" people. Thus this use of the term designates not only common sense factual beliefs ("where there's smoke, there's fire," etc.) but also certain practices (such as getting out of the rain, eating properly, etc.) and various widely held values (health, longevity, comfort, etc.). David Swenson has stated that this is *the* sense in which the term 'reason' (or 'Reason') is used, not only in the third chapter of the *Fragments*, but throughout the book.[3] I would agree that this is one of the main senses in which the term is employed by Kierkegaard's author, but as I already mentioned, I also hold that the term is used in the logical sense. I am aware of the fact that some have not recognized this sense of the term in the *Fragments*.

[3] Second edition, 1962, p. 222.

I believe that it will be clear that it is a primary sense if we turn now to a consideration of various uses of 'paradox' (including those which are emphasized by Kierkegaard's author).

Again, I should like to distinguish four different senses of the term 'paradox'. And once more, for convenience, I shall label these as the Logical, Literary, Existential, and Behavioral senses of the term.

(1) Logical paradox. In the strictest sense of the term, a logical paradox is a logical self-contradiction. This use would designate any affirmation of both a proposition, p, and its negation, $not\text{-}p$, as being true at once. In a slightly extended use, the term would also cover a set of statements which at least implicitly contain a self-contradiction or yield a self-contradictory result. Upon a superficial reading, this strict sense might seem (and has appeared to some) to be the sense in which the term is employed by Kierkegaard's author in the third chapter (and elsewhere) in the *Fragments*. But I believe that a close reading cannot support such a view. Whatever the paradox of this work is, it does not consist in the assertion of a self-contradiction or in a contradictory reality (whatever that might be).

(2) Literary paradox. By a literary paradox I mean a literary device, the use of images or descriptions in order to create a shock or *seeming* contradiction. But the contradiction is merely apparent, not actual. (Of course, as employed by some writers it *could* be actual. But the point is: it need not be.) Some of the poems of John Donne or the novels of Dostoevsky exemplify this sort of paradox. It is clear that Kierkegaard's author does not refer to this sort of paradox, even if he may come close on occasions to using such devices. He could very well do the latter without claiming that the paradox with which he is concerned is merely a literary device. Indeed, to interpret Climacus' paradox in this manner not only has no sound textual basis; it would also trivialize the whole discussion. The author is not engaged in a work of literary criticism! He addresses himself to a matter of great substance – in fact, one which he holds to be of supreme importance for one's life as a human being.

(3) Existential paradox. By an existential paradox I am referring to what one might call (and some have called) the paradox of *thought* in relation to *existence*. This notion can be elucidated by discussing a certain philosophical position. According to this "theory," all statements about matters of fact *claim* to be about that which cannot be grasped by reflection (or any other awareness). Our reflection on such matters of fact encounters that which is not amenable to reflection,

namely, existence. E.g., suppose I assert, 'This wall is green'. My statement predicates a characteristic of something, but it *presupposes* that there exists that something which we call a wall. The statement *says* that the wall is green. But in order for it to be a significant report on the world, one must presuppose more than the statement says, namely, that there *is* a wall. The term 'paradox' (in this sense) refers to this fact that existence is not a property given to reflection; rather reflection presupposes existence. Hence, any attempt to *prove* that something exists fails. Proofs have to do only with the qualities of things, *supposing* that they exist. A paradox in this sense is a limit to reflection. It is evident that Kierkegaard's author uses the term 'paradox' in this sense. We may see this most clearly in the passages of the third chapter which refer to attempts to prove the existence of God (pp. 49–56). In the author's view, such attempts are ludicrous. All that reason can do is clarify the *concept* of God, but in so doing it presupposes his existence. However, it appears that the author maintains that this is true for all existential claims.

(4) Behavioral paradox. By a behavioral paradox I mean a disturbing encounter with a set of values which conflict with one's own values. For example, as I mentioned above, most of us perhaps hold certain values to be natural or reasonable – such values as health, wealth, a long life, comfort, avoidance of pain, a secure job, etc. We deem these to be values which any rational man would seek. Thus, I might find it natural or reasonable to be concerned with my health (and perhaps do my exercises), to want a stereo (or quadraphonic) music system, a decent apartment, art objects, and various comforts of life. But now suppose that I encounter a man (or view) which opposes these – e.g., Wittgenstein, with his bare room and who gave away his fortune. I then experience a conflict. His view seems unreasonable. Of course, I cannot prove that it is unreasonable. It is a matter of interests. What he requires (or perhaps advocates) goes against my interests and concerns. The conflict or paradox is thus at the level of behavior, not of thought. I don't apprehend a logical contradiction. But I find myself profoundly disturbed at the level of my passions and concerns. This sort of paradox is also one which is of chief importance to Kierkegaard's author. The long passage on pp. 57–60 of the *Fragments* may reasonably be interpreted as pertaining to this type of paradox.

To conclude this discussion, let us then ask: What is the paradoxicality of Christianity? It has two aspects. The first consists in the fact that there is a limit to all thought. But the paradox is not solely an intellectual one. Hence, the second aspect consists in the fact that there is a conflict between our common values and interests and those which go with the person of Christ (who had no concern for a house, comfort, longevity, etc.). An opposition is set up. I am challenged to get a new set of values, to change my passions and interests. And again, in Climacus' view, there are two significant responses to the awareness of or reaction to the paradox. The first is to change my interests and concerns and to embrace those of the Christian demand. This is the happy relation of faith. The second is to say No and refuse that demand. This is the relation of offense.

Before closing this section, I anticipate at least three questions or objections.

(1) Some may ask: "But where do you find all this in the *Fragments*? I have read the book and don't see it there." This is a reasonable objection, and I believe it may be answered. The topics which are treated in the *Fragments* are presented, not only in an abstract manner, but in the words of Climacus, as a project of thought, and as a series of fragments or "scraps." It is a fairly short work at the end of which the author gives a tentative promise of a sequel, in which the "historical costume" will be provided. That sequel is the *Concluding Unscientific Postscript*, a long book which is devoted to "investing" the problem of the *Fragments* in that historical costume.[4] Thus the *Postscript* is not merely a postscript but a work which amplifies in richer detail the bare bones of the *Fragments*. As a result of this, I believe that we must read the *Fragments* in light of the *Postscript*. Upon doing so we find the explicit statement in concrete detail of what is presented in a sketchy and abstract way in the *Fragments*. (I propose to show, at least briefly, that the *Postscript* is clear with regard to one of the most crucial issues.)

(2) Others may ask: "But haven't you left out a third aspect or component of what Kierkegaard's author refers to as the Absolute Paradox, namely the Christian claim that Jesus Christ was both God and man? And doesn't this mean something more than what you have discussed? Doesn't it involve a doctrinal claim that the Eternal became temporal and that, to restate the point, Christ was both Eternal and historical? And hence is not the Paradox after all (contrary to what you have said) a logical one?" These are questions of the utmost importance. I must hence turn to them and then to an hypothesis which

4 Translated by David F. Swenson and Walter Lowrie (Princeton: Princeton University Press, 1944).

I shall propose, one which is based on the answers to those questions, and one which, in turn, I shall use as a basis for the main thesis of this chapter.

(3) Finally, someone might object to the interpretation which I have suggested on the grounds that Kierkegaard's author explicitly states that the historical fact referred to in his "story" or "project of thought," namely the fact that "God *has been*" or "God has come into existence," is a fact "based on a self-contradiction" (p. 108; also p. 109). This objection, which is closely related to the second, is also a most important one and must be adequately dealt with. However, if the second question can be adequately answered, then I believe that this one can be so answered as well. For if we can supply a satisfactory answer to the second, then this would entail that the fact referred to, even if seemingly "based on a self-contradiction," is not itself self-contradictory. Hence the questions raised in the second objection are the ones on which I shall concentrate first.

IV

I turn, then, to the questions which were raised in the second objection, at the end of the previous section. By the 'paradox' – or at least, the 'Absolute Paradox' – does not Kierkegaard's author include, not only what I have called an existential paradox and a behavioral one, but also a *doctrinal* paradox, namely the Christian claim that a certain man, Jesus Christ, was both God and man, that is, that he was both Eternal and historical (i.e., non-Eternal)? And hence does not Kierkegaard's author hold that the Christian claim is a logical contradiction and that, therefore, in order for one to be a Christian, he must embrace a self-contradiction? Note that I have formulated these questions with regard to what is held by Kierkegaard's author (Johannes Climacus) and not with regard to what is maintained by most people or with regard to what is the "correct" view on these matters. This is, of course, necessary because of the scope of this chapter. I am, you may recall, trying to establish that Climacus was not a Theist.

I want to maintain – strange as it may seem – that the answer to the above questions is No. However, I cannot defend this answer directly. Rather, in order to support it, I must proceed in several steps. First, I shall distinguish two different sorts of claims which might be made about the historical person, Jesus Christ. One of these claims is problematic. In order to interpret that claim, I shall, second, introduce the "hypothesis" to which I referred earlier and maintain that Kierkegaard's author holds this hypothesis. Then, third, I shall show that if Climacus does hold that hypothesis, it follows that he is not a Theist, and hence that the above questions require a re-interpretation which results in the fact that, for Climacus, the answers to those questions are negative. And from this it would follow that the alleged self-contradiction referred to in the third objection is not a self-contradiction.

First, then, let us consider two different sorts of claims which might be made about the historical person, Jesus Christ, claims which I would suppose are made or held by all Christians. They may be illustrated by the following two propositions:

(a) Christ existed.

(b) Christ is (or was) God (as well as man).

(Obviously, I could have used various other statements in place of (a) – 'Christ was born in Bethlehem', etc.) Clearly (a) is, in the customary sense of the term, a factual statement, in this case an historical hypothesis. One would accept it (or reject it) on the basis of historical evidence. Hence it is no different in this regard from a proposition regarding the existence of any historical person – Socrates, Napoleon, etc. And as a factual proposition, it is subject to the usual criteria of confirmability, evidence, etc. I take it that I do not have to argue either for the fact that most people would agree with what I have said about (a) or for the fact that Kierkegaard's author himself maintains what I have said about (a). But now consider (b) – or at least, part of (b), 'Christ is God'. Obviously (b) is *not* (in its customary interpretation) a factual proposition in the sense of which (a) clearly is. It is not an historical hypothesis which could be confirmed by gathering evidence, etc. Equally obviously it is not a tautology. Again, I assume that I do not have to argue for the fact that most people who accept a traditional Christian view would agree with what I have said about (b). What sort of proposition – if any – is it? Or more specifically (for our purpose), what is the position of Kierkegaard's author (Climacus) with regard to the status of (b)?

This much is clear. For Kierkegaard's author, (b) must be accepted on faith, not by argument, evidence, etc. Hence let us first ask "what is faith?" (according to the author) and then return to a consideration of his view regarding the status of (b). (In answering the present question, I shall rely on remarks made in both the *Fragments* and the *Postscript*.)

For Kierkegaard's author: First, faith is non-noetic. It is not a knowledge-relation – although, of course, it presupposes a minimal amount of neutral historical knowledge that there once was a man named Jesus, etc. Next, to be a man of faith is to be more concerned about Christ's existence than about one's own, in the sense that one is concerned about its quality and that one is concerned to have its quality become a quality of one's own existence. Thus, the object of faith is not the teaching imparted by the Teacher, but the Teacher himself. That is, the object of faith does not consist in words uttered by Jesus or in doctrines about the Teacher; it is the Teacher himself, his mode of existence. Further, faith, then, is a happy passion, not a higher level of knowledge. It is a happy relation in which my interests and concerns and those of Christ coincide. As a result, it is attainable by the unlearned as well as the learned. In summary: since faith is passional, not intellectual, the object of faith cannot be any doctrines or propositions. Faith does not consist in believing certain propositions about Christ (or whatever); it consists in a passional relation between a disciple and the Teacher in the sense that one wishes to have the mode of existence which he exemplified become the mode of one's own existence.[5]

Let us now return to the question of the status of (b). I shall divide this question into two. First, what is a *possible* view with regard to the status of (b); and second, what is the view of Johannes Climacus with regard to the status of (b)? Accordingly, I wish to provide answers to both questions. In answer to the first I shall put forward the hypothesis to which I have referred several times which I shall now call the K-theory. And in answer to the second I shall maintain that Climacus holds the K-theory.

According to the K-theory, (b) – 'Christ is God (and man)' – is not a factual statement (in the sense discussed above). Nor is it a tautology. Nor is it a metaphysical statement about some transhistorical entity. Nor is it a theological – doctrinal statement or creedal assertion about any such entity. What, then, is it? (b) is an assertion of *passion* which says something about those who claim that Christ is God, and *not* an assertion which says that an individual who, in addition to being a man, was also non-human, "divine," etc. For those who make the claim, to utter (b) is not to say something about a certain historical person's having possessed a non-worldly attribute, etc.; rather to utter (b)

[5] See *Fragments*, pp. 61, 73, 76–77, 109, 118; *Postscript*, pp. 53, 118, 188, 290–291.

is to say something primarily about one's self, the utterer that one's self has been reorganized, reintegrated in a certain way; it is to say something primarily about one's reality as an historical person with relation to the reality of another historical person. That is, whereas the "unbeliever" holds "My interest in my existence is my reality," the man of faith holds "My interest in Christ's existence is my reality." And to say the latter is to say that what constitutes my reality is the fact that my chief passions and concerns are the passions and concerns exemplified by Christ, that I have transformed my mode of existence into the mode of Christ's existence, and that as a result I have found new meaning and purpose in my own life. Thus, according to the K-theory, (b) is not to be interpreted along the lines of traditional theological doctrines as referring to some non-natural, trans-historical entity or attribute. It is to be interpreted as expressing something subjectively extraordinary about something very ordinary, that is, that one's existence has meaning only when one lives a new kind of life.

So much for the K-theory and the answer to the first of the above two questions. It may be recalled that I said, in answer to the second, that Johannes Climacus holds the K-theory. Now, clearly, if Climacus holds the K-theory, then it follows that: first, Climacus was not a Theist; and second, that his notion of the Paradox does not involve any doctrinal paradox or self-contradiction. For if Climacus holds the K-theory, then his references to God, the Eternal, etc., are not made with regard to any traditionally conceived transcendent being (or attribute), but rather are references to human beings and their passional relations to another human being whose existence became a model for those others and thereby transformed their mode of existence. All such discourse is about entities and characteristics within the natural world; none of it is about any transcendent or other-worldly entities or characteristics. Thus once again, if Climacus holds the K-theory, then my main thesis has been defended: Johannes Climacus was not a Theist. And from this it follows that his notion of the Paradox does not involve any doctrinal component (about two "natures," the Eternal versus the historical, etc.) and that it does not involve any self-contradiction. For again, concepts such as *God*, *Eternal*, etc., are all given an interpretation whereby what seemed to be contradictory is not. Hence, if Climacus holds the K-theory, then the objections which were raised are readily answered and are not genuine objections.

All of this of course assumes that Climacus holds the K-theory. But *does* he hold the K-theory? I have already tried to suggest that there is evidence for the views developed in this paper in the *Fragments*, but I said that, for more conclusive evidence, we must turn to the *Postscript*. Similarly, I believe that there are suggestions that Climacus holds the K-theory in the *Fragments* but that more conclusive evidence may be found in the *Postscript*. Hence, in order to defend the theses that Climacus held the K-theory and that therefore he was not a Theist, we must now turn to the *Postscript*.

v

Before turning to passages from the *Postscript*, let me summarize what I take to be some of the main themes concerning the problems with which we are here concerned – themes which are suggested in the *Fragments* and amplified in the *Postscript*. 'Christ is God' is not an historical hypothesis about Christ, in the sense in which 'Christ existed' is such an hypothesis. Nor is it a metaphysical or doctrinal claim about a transcendent being or attribute. It is rather, an assertion of passion and interest about the individual who makes that claim, namely that he has found a new life, a life in which the various factors of his personality, his interests and concerns have found a new synthesis. To say that 'Jesus Christ is God' is to say that Jesus Christ is that person who maximizes one's interests and passions in a unique way which has transformed one's existence.

I shall now quote some of the passages from the *Postscript* which are most relevant to the main themes of this paper.

(1) In the Introduction to the volume, Kierkegaard's author restates the questions asked on the title page of the *Fragments* and the answers thereto. He then says:

But in order to avoid confusion, it is at once necessary to recall that our treatment of the problem does not raise the question of the truth of Christianity. It merely deals with the question of the individual's relationship to Christianity (pp. 18–19).[6]

(2) A bit later we read:

In Christianity ... the truth is the subject's transformation in himself (pp. 37–38).

[6] Page numbers in parentheses in this section refer to the edition of the *Postscript* cited above.

(3) And a few pages later:

In relation to Christianity ... objectivity is a most unfortunate category ... for Christianity is precisely an affair of spirit, and so of subjectivity, and so of inwardness (p. 42).

(4) And still later:

If Christianity is essentially subjectivity, it is a mistake for the observer to be objective. In every case where the object of knowledge is the very inwardness of the subjectivity of the individual, it is necessary for the knower to be in a corresponding condition (p. 51).

(5) Similarly:

Christianity does not lend itself to objective observation, precisely because it proposes to intensify subjectivity to the utmost (p. 55).

(6) I turn now to some of the most important passages of all. For example:

When the question of truth is raised in an objective manner, reflection is directed objectively to the truth, as an object to which the knower is related. Reflection is not focused upon the relationship, however, but upon the question of whether it is the truth to which the knower is related. If only the object to which he is related is the truth, the subject is accounted to be in the truth. When the question of truth is raised subjectively, reflection is directed subjectively to the nature of the individual's relationship: if only the mode of this relationship is in the truth, the individual is in the truth even if he should happen to be thus related to what is not true. Let us take as an example the knowledge of God. Objectively, reflection is directed to the problem of whether this object is the true God; subjectively, reflection is directed to the question whether the individual is related to a *something in such a manner* that his relationship is in truth a God-relationship (p. 178).

(7) Or consider this amazing passage:

If one who lives in the midst of Christendom goes up to the house of God, the house of the true God, with the conception of God in his knowledge, and prays, but prays in a false spirit; and one who lives in an idolatrous community prays with the entire passion of the infinite, although his eyes rest upon an idol: where is there most truth? The one (the latter) prays in truth to God though he worships an idol; the other (the former) prays falsely to the true God, and hence worships in fact an idol (pp. 179–80).

(8) And later:

(God) is in the creation, and present everywhere in it, but directly He is not there; and only when the individual turns to his inner self, and hence only in the inwardness of self-activity, does he have his attention aroused, and is enabled to see God (p. 218).

(9) Or consider the following:

The difficulty facing an existing individual is how to give his existence the continuity without which everything simply vanishes ... The goal of movement for an existing individual is to arrive at a decision, and to renew it. The eternal is the factor of continuity; but an abstract eternity is extraneous to the movement of life, and a concrete eternity within the existing individual is the maximum degree of his passion (p. 277).

(10) And later:

Existence is the highest interest of the existing individual, and his interest in his existence constitutes his reality (p. 279).

(11) And, related to this:

The believer differs from the ethicist in being infinitely interested in the reality of another (p. 288).

(12) And finally:

A believer is one who is infinitely interested in another's reality. This is a decisive criterion for faith ... the object of faith is the reality of another, and the relationship is one of infinite interest. The object of faith is not a doctrine ... The object of faith is the reality of the teacher ... Christianity is no doctrine concerning the unity of the divine and the human, or concerning the identity of subject and object; nor is it any other of the logical transcriptions of Christianity ... Faith constitutes a sphere all by itself, and every misunderstanding of Christianity may at once be recognized by its transforming it into a doctrine ... The maximum of attainment within the sphere of faith is to become infinitely interested in the reality of the teacher (pp. 290–01).

I shall not comment on or analyze these passages (or others which could have been quoted). I shall simply say that I believe that the key to interpreting them lies especially in (6) and (7), and that if we are to take these remarks seriously, then the following seems to me to be true: When Climacus uses terms such as 'God', 'Paradox', 'eternal', 'infinite', he employs them in a most unusual way. His uses of these and related expressions do not refer to any transcendent entities or attributes. Rather they refer to certain concrete objects and characteristics in the world – human beings and their mode of existence. Thus, to take one example, the term 'eternal' does not for Climacus refer to a state of everlastingness or to a realm or state which is opposed to the realm of the historical. Rather, it refers to a certain quality of one's existence here and now, in this life, if he has become a man of faith. Similarly for other expressions.

As a result of our interpretation of these passages, let us return to claim that Christ was God and man. What is meant by 'God' here and what is meant by 'faith in God'? It seems clear that Climacus holds that God is not some unique transcendent entity. Rather God is anything, for anyone, that can captivate and control his interests, passions, and concerns. And one becomes a religious man, a man of faith, in virtue of the character of his interests and concerns. Climacus claims that, among the large number of historical existents which are capable of being "believed in" (that is, embraced passionally in faith), only one allows for a synthesis of the factors of one's personality which is capable of making one into a new creature, and that is the historical man, Jesus Christ. To say that he is God and to say that he is one who can captivate and sustain human interests and concerns in such a way that one who embraces the mode of existence which he presented finds that all things are "made new." Again, whereas, prior to such acceptance, one maintained that his interest in his own existence is his reality, he now finds that his interest in Christ's existence is his reality. And this is why *Christ is called God*. Needless to say, this is a view which is far different from that of traditional Theism.

Hence, I believe that I have established that Johannes Climacus did hold the K-theory and that consequently he was not a Theist. It is, I think, a remarkable achievement on the part of Kierkegaard to have, via his pseudonymous author, proposed an interpretation of Christianity which is not only unorthodox but astonishingly original.

VI

But what about Kierkegaard himself? Is it reasonable to suppose that he himself was not a Theist? In the "Declaration" at the end of the *Postscript* he says that, "in the pseudonymous works there is not a single word which is mine" (p. 551). However, there is a brief passage in *The Point of View*[7] which makes one wonder. He divides his writings into three groups: (1) the aesthetic works, which include all the pseudonymous works except the *Postscript* (and also 18 edifying discourses); (2) the *Postscript*; and (3) the religious works, the later writings such as *The Works of Love*, etc. He then says that the first group is aesthetic, that the third group is "exclusively religious," and that "between them, as the turning-point," lies the *Postscript*. He then writes: *"The Concluding Postscript* is not an aesthetic work, but neither is it in the strictest sense religious. Hence it is by a pseudonym, though I add my name

---

[7] Translated by Walter Lowrie (London: Oxford University Press, 1939) p. 13.

as editor – a thing I did not do in the case of any purely aesthetic work. This is a hint for him who is concerned about such things and has a flair for them."

O, enigmatic and mysterious Dane – hiding behind or concealed within your pseudonyms, prefaces, introductions, appendices, first and last declarations, and points of views, pleading that we not lay a dialectic hand upon your work, but let it stand – have you perpetuated a gigantic hoax and then retired to your chamber in which you gazed out the window and, noting the spectacle of scholars, translators, and interpreters who have wrestled with your words, responded with a gale of uproarious laughter?

CHAPTER VI

KIERKEGAARD'S VIEWS ON CHRISTIANITY

In the previous chapters I have focused upon more theoretical aspects
of Kierkegaard's thought. In this final chapter I shall discuss an issue
which, although it is in part a theoretical one, is also a more "practical"
one: Kierkegaard's views on Christianity. As we shall see, perhaps a
more accurate formulation of the title might be: Kierkegaard's views
of Christendom versus Christianity.[1]

I

In March, 1855, Kierkegaard wrote:

The religious situation in our country is: Christianity (that is, the Christianity
of the New Testament – and everything else is not Christianity . . .), Christianity
does not exist . . .
    We have a complete crew of bishops, deans, and priests; learned men, eminent-
ly learned, talented, gifted, humanly well-meaning; they all declaim . . . but
not one of them is in the character of the New Testament. But if such is the case,
the existence of this Christian crew is so far from being, Christianly considered,
advantageous to Christianity that it is far rather a peril, because it is so infinitely
likely to give rise to a false impression . . . that when we have such a crew we
must of course have Christianity too . . .
    We are what is called a 'Christian' nation – but . . . not a single one of us is in
the character of the Christianity of the New Testament . . . The illusion of a
Christian nation is due doubtless to the power which number exercises over the
imagination . . . They tell a ludicrous story about an innkeeper . . . It is said
that he sold his beer by the bottle for a cent less than he paid for it; and when
a certain man said to him, 'How does that balance the account? That means
to spend money,' he replied, 'No, my friend it's the big number that does it' . . .
So also with the calculation which arrives at a Christian nation by adding up

---

[1] Except for quoted passages, most of my comments in this chapter are based on Kierkegaard's *Concluding Unscientific Postscript*, and some of the later religious writings, especially
Training in Christianity.

units which are not Christian, getting the result by means of the notion that the big number does it ...

O Luther, thou hadst 95 theses – terrible! ... This case is far more terrible: there is only one thesis.

The Christianity of the New Testament simply does not exist.[2]

These are but two of dozens of similar passages which Kierkegaard wrote in 1854–55. What prompted such outbursts? There is, undoubtedly, no single fact which can explain them other than the fact which Kierkegaard purported to describe: the non-existence of Christianity. However (as is well known) there is an incident which served as the occasion for some of these vehement writings. A certain Bishop Mynster who ruled the Church of Denmark for many years died in 1853. Shortly after his death a Professor Martenson preached a memorial sermon in which he eulogized the late bishop as "yet one more link in the holy chain of witnesses for the truth, stretching from the days of the Apostles unto our own time." This idealization of Mynster seemed to Kierkegaard to be a complete falsification of Christian categories. For after all, here was a man who had lived in a mansion, had servants to wait upon him, etc. Hence, Kierkegaard wrote a passionate protest in 1854 entitled "Was Bishop Mynster a 'witness to the truth'?" in which he gives a negative answer and his reason for it.

A witness to the truth is a man whose life from first to last is unacquainted with everything which is called enjoyment ... (Rather) from first to last it was initiated into what is called suffering ... by inward conflicts, by fear and trembling, by trepidation, by anguish of soul, by agony of spirit, being tried besides that by all the sufferings which are more commonly talked of in the world. A witness to the truth is a man who in poverty witnesses to the truth – in poverty, in lowliness, in abasement, and so is unappreciated, hated, abhorred, and then derided, insulted, mocked ... then at last crucified, or beheaded, or burnt.[3]

Kierkegaard's attack caused a sensation and aroused a storm of protest. He was accused of attacking the memory of the dead. But he cast aside all of these objections and kept hammering at his theme in *The Fatherland*. In fact, since he was not concerned merely with Bishop Mynster, he enlarged it to include all of Christendom. His main theme was: what passed for the Christianity of the New Testament in the established Church was not the Christianity of the New Testament as exemplified in Christ and the Apostles.

[2] *Kierkegaard's Attack Upon Christendom*. Transl. by W. Lowrie (Princeton: Princeton University Press, 1946), pp. 29–32.
[3] *Ibid.*, p. 7.

Throughout several months of 1855, in the journal, *The Instant*, Kierkegaard elaborated on his main theme: Christianity did not exist in Christendom. The articles became more and more forceful and continued to stress what Kierkegaard had said at the end of 1854:

This has to be said; so be it now said.
   Whoever thou art, ... by ceasing to take part (if ordinarily thou dost) in the public worship of God, as it now is (with the claim that it is the Christianity of the New Testament), thou hast constantly one guilt the less: thou dost not take part in treating God as a fool by calling that the Christianity of the New Testament which is not the Christianity of the New Testament.[4]

People hounded him. What was he driving at? Kierkegaard answered: "Quite simply: I want honesty."[5] The end came soon after. He died in November, 1855.

II

Kierkegaard maintained that Christianity did not exist in Christendom. What, then, was his conception of Christianity? This question has many facets. I propose to emphasize one of them: Kierkegaard's view of what it means to be a Christian.

   Let us begin by first stating what (in Kierkegaard's view) Christianity is *not*. Christianity is not simply the conveying of an intellectual content. Being a Christian is not the same as having a view of life or having certain doctrines about God, Christ, etc. Thus knowing more and more theology does not necessarily enhance one's personal religiosity. Further, Christianity is not simply a matter of willing. If it were, there would be no way of distinguishing religiosity from wish-fulfillment. Similarly, Christianity is not simply a matter of emotions. In short, Christianity is no *one* thing.

   Let us then turn to what (according to Kierkegaard) Christianity *is*. In his view, Christianity proposes a possibility – what Paul L. Holmer has often called a new synthesis of one's entire personality, a refashioning of one's existence in a new way, a re-integration, which is called salvation. Thus the only thing that can be Christian is a person; a church or society, etc., cannot. The only appropriate referent to which the term 'Christian' should be applied is a personality – one who is re-integrated, born again, made new. The integration here is at the

---

[4] *Ibid.*, p. 59.
[5] *Ibid.*, p. 41.

level of one's existence; it is not an integration of words, thoughts or propositions. Thus, when Christianity speaks of faith, the proper object of faith is a person and not a proposition or doctrine. The Apostle said, "We preach Christ Jesus and him crucified," not propositions about him. For one can grasp propositions and yet escape the personal integration and thereby miss the essential thing: the new synthesis of personality. Of course, such re-integration is never fully achieved. A human being is in a process of change. Hence the synthesis must be reaffirmed constantly, and the task is never finished until the hour of one's death.

Now, of course, Christianity involves both a *view* of existing and a *way* of existing. But Christianity, if grasped only as a view of existing, is not genuine Christianity. In order to become a Christian, one must also grasp it as a way of existing. As a result of this dual aspect, Christianity is something which can be conceived and understood before it is realized. Thus it can be talked about and be the subject of preaching or teaching. We can discourse about Christianity and our discourse can be objective, logical, and rational. But there is a difference between Christian teaching or preaching and teaching in the more standard sense. In the case of the latter, all that is required is that one conceive and understand the thought that is conveyed in the teaching. But in the case of Christian teaching, more is involved. The perfection of the Christian life comes not when one understands what is conveyed in the teaching but when one goes out and realizes it in one's existence.

This means that Christianity always has an ethical-behavorial component. As the New Testament asks: "What do ye more than others?" If this ethical component is omitted, the result, as Kierkegaard sees it, is a mere collection of myths (about Adam and Eve, etc.) or a group of doctrines (about the two natures of Christ, etc.). To avoid falling into these errors, the ethical component must be stressed. The something-to-be-done aspect of Christian faith is essential. It was Kierkegaard's chief aim to stress that it is getting lost in Christendom.

And what is it that one must do? What is the Christian task? To imitate Christ. To do as he did, to deny one's self, take up one's cross, and follow him. As Kierkegaard said:

(Suppose) a man dies and leaves his whole fortune to an heir – but there is a condition, something which is required of the heir, and this the heir does not like. What then does he do? He takes possession of the property (for he is indeed the heir, says he) and says good-day to the obligation.
This, as everybody knows, is dishonesty ...

So it is with 'Christendom' ... It is devised to mankind by the Testament of the Savior of the world; but in the case of Christianity, the situation is this: the gift and the obligation correspond to one another in an exact proportion. In the same degree that Christianity is a gift it is also an obligation.

The knavish trick of 'Christendom' is to take the gift and say good-day to the obligation ...

However, hypocritical as everything is with 'Christendom', they have made it appear as if Christendom too did maintain that Christianity is an obligation – one has to be baptized. Ah! That is making confoundedly short work of obligation! A drop of water on the head of an infant, in the name of the Trinity – that is obligation!

No, obligation is: the imitation of Jesus Christ.[6]

III

Finally, in the light of all this, we may ask: What is the task of Christian teaching? According to Kierkegaard, there are two main types of dialectic by which communication takes place. One has been called the *noetic* dialectic. Essential to this dialectic are the distinctions between knowledge and ignorance and between truth and falsity. This is the dialectic employed by most teaching, scholarship and science in order to obtain more information or in order to understand a given subject matter. It of course can be applied to activities related to Christianity, for example, in order to obtain more historical information about the apostle Paul or about the formation and development of the Church. But, according to Kierkegaard, Christianity emphasizes the need for a second dialectic, the *religious* dialectic. Essential to this dialectic is the distinction between faith and doubt, not that between knowledge and ignorance. What is of concern here is not to reduce ignorance and increase knowledge, but to reduce doubt and increase faith.

There are two main tasks or components of Christian teaching which operate within the religious dialectic. First, such teaching must show the various alternative modes of existence which are available to men to let the individual choose which among them he wishes to actualize. Christian teaching should portray all possible existential alternatives and allow the individual to make his own choice, a choice which at once is an act of faith and a resolution of doubt. Among these alternatives is that of Christianity, which stresses the mode of existence embodied in Christ. But again, this mode must be portrayed as one

---

[6] *Ibid.*, p. 280.

among many. Some may reject it. Others may come to accept it in faith, which, once more, is not a belief in propositions or doctrines, but the passionate, existential appropriation of a possibility. Second, Christian teaching (according to Kierkegaard) should also call attention to the illusions imbedded in our culture and to which individuals cling. The task here is to show that the illusions may not be worth embracing because they are not capable of serving as ultimate ends or objects of faith. The interests and passions of men are often captivated by these transitory illusions. Christian teaching should make them aware of a concern which is worthy of their passion and interest. As Kierkegaard has often stressed: People have an infinite passion for the finite; what they need is an infinite passion for the infinite.[7]

---

[7] In the above, as throughout this volume, I am greatly indebted to Paul L. Holmer.

ACKNOWLEDGEMENTS

I am grateful to the editors and publishers who kindly granted per-
mission to reprint (in a revised form) the following papers:

Ch. II. "Logicality Versus Alogicality in the Christian Faith," *The
    Journal of Religion*, 38 (1958), 107–15.

Ch. III. "Some Insights for Ethical Theory from Kierkegaard," *The

Ch.

N. E.

I.

ul?" *The Journal of*